Scottish BATTLES

"Scottish Battles" was published in 1985 by Lang Syne Publishers Ltd., Newtongrange, Midlothian, and printed by Waterside Printers, Old School, Blanefield, Glasgow. This is a reprint of the original edition published by Brown, Son and Ferguson of Glasgow. Produced by arrangement with the original publishers and protected by copyright. The illustrations by John Mackay © LANG SYNE PUBLISHERS LTD. are published here for the first time.
I.S.B.N. 0 946264 80 5.

introduction

WHILE this book may be accepted with confidence as a reliable volume of reference concerning all the campaigns in which Scottish troops have been engaged, and the battles they have fought from Mons Graupius to Culloden, it is intended primarily for the general reader who wants a clear concise account of Scotland's military history.

All the campaigns are included, and the principal battles are described in considerable detail, together with a survey of the political events which led to war and of the social and economic conditions of Scotland at the various periods.

Of particular interest are the pen portraits of the military leaders and famous soldiers who from time to time have arisen in our country, the studies of methods of fighting and of Scottish troops in the different phases of their development as instruments of warfare.

The book is well indexed, and, although only those wars which had a direct bearing on subsequent history are gone into in full detail, a sufficient amount of information is given about every battle fought on Scottish soil or by Scottish soldiers in England or France.

At Mons Graupius in the begining — or to be precise A.D.86 — an army of 30,000 Caledonians faced the invading Romans. They were a federation of tribes which had been formed under the leadership of a mighty warrior named Calgacus.

Later came struggles against Viking warriors with such fearsome names as "Eric the Red Axe", "Cleaver of Skulls" and "Brainspiller".

These men made lightning raids from beaches. They spread rapidly throughout the countryside killing burning and looting before returning to their ships laden with spoils.

But it was in conflicts against the English that rivers of blood flowed for centuries. Bannockburn was our greatest victory followed by Stirling Bridge. Thirdly, and perhaps less well remembered, came Baugé in Normandy where 1700 Englishmen fell.

Other points which emerge from the book include:—

★ How an English Queen's plea as "a damsel in distress" led to the death of the Scottish king, his son and 10,000 subjects including 13 earls, 15 lords and an archbishop.

★ How the Battle of Pinkie was one of the darkest blots on the page of Scottish history. It was the only occasion where an army fled in terror before the enemy had barely struck a blow.

★ Civil wars: but of the many battles in which Scot fought against Scot perhaps the only one which can claim to have exercised decisive influence on the nation's fortunes was Langside.

★ The day four thousand men were expelled from the Scottish army for 'lack of godliness' and the subsequent religious lunacy which led to 3,000 others being killed and 10,000 taken prisoner.

★ How the horror of the Covenanting troubles took a dramatic turn when the eyes, tongue, mouth, nose and ears were torn from a corpse in a case of mistaken identity.

★ The momentous declaration made by the Scottish Parliament in 1689 which was to cost Scotland many lives.

★ Even after the Union in 1707 there was still trouble caused by the English majority in Parliament who violated practically every clause in the agreement. The laws of Scotland were set aside; the liberties of her church were infringed; her industries were stifled; and our courts were subjected to the control of an English assembly.

★ How Bonnie Prince Charlie won victory at Prestonpans where his men killed 400 enemy troops and took a further 700 prisoner. All the dragoons, through cowardice, escaped.

★ Defeat for the Prince at Culloden. His troops were half starved having been on short rations for weeks. That morning of the battle they'd had one tiny bannock apiece which was of the coarsest bread. Afterwards the victorious troops roamed over the battlefields bayoneting in cold blood every wounded Highlander who lay helpless at their feet, while the dragoons cut down every fugitive they could find.

For four miles the road to Inverness was strewn with mangled corpses.

the 12ᵗʰ century — 13ᵗʰ century — and early 14ᵗʰ century —

...tury — 18ᵗʰ century — Government troops & The Highlander —

Caledonian Alliance versus the Romans!

MONS GRAUPIUS.

(A.D. 86)

IT was in the year 80 of the Christian era that the country which was to become Scotland emerged from the mists of unrecorded time, and found its first place in history as the scene of the later exploits in Britain of Agricola, the Roman general who had the good fortune, or the shrewd foresight, to have for son-in-law the most brilliant historian of his days. Had Tacitus not come north with his pen and his parchments, the story of Scotland would not have begun till some centuries later than it did.

In 78, Agricola had landed in South Britain, almost the whole of which he found already subdued and peacefully settled as part of the Roman Empire. Only the Cymri of Wales were still holding out against the invaders. A single summer campaign, in 79, sufficed to see them, too, brought under the yoke. In the following year Agricola began his march to the north, with Tacitus installed as official chronicler of his triumphant progress.

What route he followed is unknown; but it may be assumed almost with certainty that it was the road so often trod in after ages by other armies on the same errand. Keeping in touch with his ships which were skirting the coast, he would keep his troops always within sight and easy reach of the sea, moving them along the paths which linked the rude beginnings of Berwick, Dunbar and Edinburgh.

He crossed the Forth, and penetrated as far as the Tay. It was no easy journey he had. The natives were accustomed to war, and well armed with bows and spears. In place of cavalry they had their battle-

1

chariots, with sharpened blades projecting from the hubs, terrible weapons when driven at speed against the foe, shearing through limbs like scythes through standing corn.

On the line of the Tay, and the lochs that lie beyond it to the west, the Romans halted for a season, maintaining themselves in fortified camps throughout the winter, while the Caledonians—such was the name Tacitus bestowed on our forebears—harassed them continually, raiding outposts, cutting off convoys, slitting the throats of unfortunate stragglers, practising, in short, to perfection all the arts of guerilla warfare in which they were adept.

It was a trying winter for Agricola and his legions, but they saw it through. In the spring the general decided to provide himself with a more secure line of defence. He did not abandon his advanced camps; but behind them he constructed a chain of forts, at intervals of two or three miles, right across the country from the firth of Forth to the firth of Clyde. This occupied his second summer in Caledonia. The cautious slowness of the Roman campaign, under a skilful and by no means timid commander, is a tribute to the military prowess of our ancestors.

In the following year Agricola ventured beyond the Clyde. He entered Cowal and Argyll, explored the west coast for some little distance, and had a sight of the Hebrides. It was no more than a scouting expedition, however, a reconnaissance in force. Before the snows of winter he was wisely back behind his forts again.

Meanwhile the Caledonians had not been idle. They were not a nation, probably not even all of one race, but were divided into many tribes, each proud of its independence. Their early efforts at resistance to the invaders were, therefore, disconnected and ineffective; but they soon came to realise that only by standing together could they hope to keep their liberty. They formed a federation, and chose a famous chief, a mighty warrior named Galgacus, to be their leader.

maintained scattered fortresses further north and even built a lesser wall between the Forth and the Clyde, but their hold on any part of Caledonia was always precarious in the extreme. They were constantly engaged in a guerilla warfare with the natives, and finally they were compelled to abandon the whole territory to its indomitable owners.

It is no empty boast of the Scots that of all the countries in Europe invaded by the legions of Rome, theirs is the only one in which the Empire utterly failed in its attempt at conquest.

Dunnichen (Nectansmere) (20th May, 685).—The country inhabited by our forefathers was for long divided into several kingdoms. There were Pictland, between the Forth and the Spey; Dalriada (Scots), represented to-day by Argyll; and Strathclyde (Britons), stretching from the Solway to the Clyde. The western isles and most of the north-west of the mainland were in the hands of the Norwegian ruler of the Orkneys; while the south-east, from the Tweed to the Forth, formed part of the Anglo-Danish kingdom of Northumbria.

The most powerful of the native kingdoms was Pictland. The Picts were a virile and warlike race, the descendants of the followers of Galgacus, and they were in almost constant strife with their English neighbours, who were consumed with an ambition to extend their border to the Tay.

In the year 685 the most determined attempt to achieve this aim was made by Ecgfrith of Northumbria, who led an army across the Forth at Stirling, and pushed on through Perthshire to the Tay. The Picts fell back before the invaders, drawing them into the deeper recesses of the hills, and at the same time gradually surrounding them. At Dunnichen, in Angus, the trap closed on the Angles. The Picts fell on them from all sides. Ecgfrith was slain, and his army was routed with fearful slaughter.

How silver cross in sky became battle standard

THE tale of " the Silver Cross to Scotland dear" goes back, if the legend be true, more than eleven hundred years. Its first appearance on a battlefield, over Scottish troops, was, so we are told, the sign of the intervention of heaven on the side of our forebears.

The story is told by George Buchanan in his *History of Scotland*.

About the beginning of the ninth century, when our country was still divided into several little kingdoms, the southern Picts were at variance with the people of Northumbria, whose king at the time was a Danish chief named Athelstane. Hungus, the king of the Picts, resolved to carry war into his enemy's territory; so, his force strengthened by the addition of a considerable body of men lent him by his brother-in-law Achaius, king of the Scots, he marched boldly into Northumbria, spreading a trail of fire and blood across the country.

Athelstane was a brave warrior, who feared neither Pict nor Scot. Gathering his forces, he set off in pursuit of Hungus, who was now retiring with an immense store of plunder, to his own fastnesses. Near Haddington the two armies came face to face.

The Picts were taken by surprise, and were outnumbered by their foes; yet for a whole day they maintained themselves stubbornly against the furious onset of the southern spears. Night fell at last. The fires were lit and the watches set, and the two forces, battle-worn and weary, laid themselves down to sleep.

But for Hungus, exhausted though he was by the toils and alarms of the day, there was to be little rest. He realised that his army was in deadly peril, from which only the help of God and His saints might safely withdraw

8

it, so he set himself to spend the night in prayer and earnest supplication for Divine assistance on the morrow.

Before day broke he fell into a slumber, and in it there appeared to him Andrew the apostle, who bade him be of good courage and promised that a glorious victory would be given to him and his people.

When Hungus awoke, he caused the news of his vision to be told to all his men. The promise of the saint put new heart into them, and filled them with resolution to do their part to their utmost in the coming fray.

That day was occupied with skirmishing and affairs of outposts, while the main bodies of the two armies rested and prepared themselves for the general engagement which they knew would commence on the following daybreak.

When at length they stood face to face, the Picts and Northumbrians, in battle array and eager for the conflict, a great cross of shining silver appeared in the sky, the cross of Saint Andrew. It was the token that the promise made to Hungus was to be fulfilled.

The men of the south were struck with dismay by this heavenly apparition; the Picts were elated and inspired, and fought like men possessed. The battle quickly became a rout, in which the Northumbrian army was cut to pieces. Its leader was killed, and the battlefield was called after him Athelstaneford, the name which it bears to this day.

After so signal a manifestation of his good-will, it is small wonder that Andrew was accepted as the patron saint of the Picts, and later of united Scotland, and that his cross became the battle standard of the nation.

It may be a fable, the story of Hungus; but one fact is certain. From the time of the earliest records, when Scottish troops went into battle, it was with a silver cross on an azure field floating over them, while their cry was ever, "God and Saint Andrew! Saint Andrew for Scotland!" That flag was shewn and that cry resounded at Stirling Bridge, at Bannockburn and on the dark day of Flodden; in France, when Scottish breasts were forming a living wall round Joan of Arc; wherever Scottish lives were gladly given for Scotland's honour. When the last Scottish force was shattered at Culloden, it was the silver cross that was drenched with the blood of the clans.

BRUNANBURH (937).—For three years a confederation of Scots, Strathclyde Britons and Northumbrian Danes waged a war against Athelstan, the most powerful of the kings of Saxon England. The allies were finally defeated at Brunanburh, an unidentified locality, whose site is usually placed somewhere in Dumfriesshire.

DUNCANSNESS (994).—In the reign of Kenneth II, a Norwegian jarl of Orkney, Sigurd the Stout, laid claim to the earldom of Caithness, which he invaded with a large force of Norsemen. He was met by a Scottish army at Duncansness. Sigurd was victorious in the fight, but his losses had been so great that he retired to his own territory and abandoned his claim.

MORTLACH (1010).—For several years a large part of the north of Scotland had been overrun by the Danes. In a fiercely contested battle, they were defeated at Mortlach, in Banffshire, by Malcolm II.

CARHAM (1018).—The Anglo-Danes of Northumbria for long claimed possession of the territory between the Tweed and the Forth. They were finally driven out of it by Malcolm II, who inflicted on them a crushing defeat at Carham on the Tweed, one of the most momentous battles in Scottish history, ranking in importance with Bannockburn.

LUMPHANAN (1057).—When Macbeth, an able ruler with a legitimate claim to the throne, had reigned for seventeen years, a rising took place under Malcolm, the natural son of the previous king, Duncan. At Lumphanan, in Aberdeenshire, Macbeth was defeated and slain, and his rival became Malcolm III (Canmore).

to meet the Scots in the field. The first thing they did was to engage the assistance of all the saints of the north of England. On a waggon they erected a tall mast, which was hung around with holy relics and crowned with the banners of St. Peter of York, St. John of Beverley, St. Wilfred of Ripon and St. Cuthbert, for even the departed knights of the Church were given armorial bearings in those feudal days, and enlisted in the service of their devotees. Cuthbert might have been thought a risky choice. Although his mortal remains lay now in Durham, he was born in Lothian and had been a monk of Melrose; but events were to prove his loyalty to the country of his posthumous adoption.

The saintly talisman was carried in the van of the English army; and around it Thurstan's warriors rallied in the engagement which has taken from it the name of the "Battle of the Standard." Before the action commenced, a box containing the consecrated host was attached to the flag-pole, "so that Jesus Christ was bodily present as commander in the battle." Blasphemous as such an idea may appear to us to-day, in twelfth century England it was the extreme of piety.

David crossed the Tees, and the two armies faced each other near the village of Northallerton. They were as different as two military forces possibly could be. The English were comparatively few in number, but were well armed and well disciplined. They consisted, for the most part, of Norman knights and barons and their retainers, clad in mail and furnished with heavy lances. There were archers also, not yet provided with the longbow which was to become England's most deadly weapon, yet stout bowmen none the less whose steel-tipped shafts would fly true and pierce deep.

The Scottish army had its knights and archers too, but these were only a small part of the whole. The majority carried the light weapons of their everyday turbulent life, and had no better protection than shields and jerkins of studded leather to ward off lance and arrow.

David's plan was that his first attack should be delivered by his men-at-arms and bowmen. "All the armed men, knights and archers whom they had were to go before the rest of the army, so that armed men should attack armed men, and knights engage with knights, and arrows resist arrows." The Picts from Galloway, however, obstinately refused to be deprived of what they claimed to be their ancient right of always fighting in the first rank of any Scottish army they might be in, and the king had perforce to submit to them. Had he been able to insist on his own scheme for the battle, the whole subsequent course of British history might have taken a very different line from what it did; but there was no arguing with men who declared that "we surely have iron sides, breasts of bronze, minds void of fear; our feet have never known flight, nor our backs a wound." In their scorn of armour the Picts were supported by one of David's greatest nobles, Malise of Strathearn, who vowed that, though he wore no mail, "he would advance further into the ranks of the enemy than those who cased themselves in steel."

The king had to alter his order of battle. The men of Galloway were placed in the centre of the front line; on their right were the mailed knights and the warriors from Cumbria and Teviotdale; on the left the Lothian men, the Highlanders and the Islesmen. The reserve consisted of the Moray men and the eastern Scots, commanded by David himself.

The English were gathered in close array around their standard, a solid wall of spears. Against them rushed the first wave of the Scots, who met with varied fortune. On the left, the commander of the wing was slain, "and his whole nation turned in flight, for God was offended, and all their valour was broken like spiders' webs." So the English chroniclers have it.

In the centre, the men of Galloway fought with all the courage of their race. An eye-witness has left an account of them. "Like a hedgehog with its quills, so would you see a Pict bristling all round with the arrows that had pierced him, yet still brandishing his sword, and in blind madness rushing forward, now smiting a foe, now beating the air with vain blows."

But the valour of half-naked men, even the most reckless, is of small account when matched against steel-clad warriors behind a hedge of spears. Again and again the Picts threw themselves on their foes, and again and again they were beaten back.

Prince Henry was in command on the right. Putting himself at the head of his band of knights and men-at-arms, he charged furiously against the English left, broke it, and drove it in confusion from the field.

For three hours of a summer day the fight continued. David brought up his reserves, and launched attack after attack on the English line. But every assault was in vain. The Scots had the courage, but they lacked the means for victory. As in one record it is quaintly put, "the frailty of the Scottish lances was mocked by the denseness of iron and wood" that walled round their enemies.

At length, realising that success was beyond his power, the king of Scots abandoned the battle and drew off his men. He had not been defeated, but only baffled, though his army had sustained tremendous losses in the bloody conflict around the Standard.

Northallerton must be ranked as a drawn battle. The English, for whom their own historians claim it as a great victory, certainly held the field; but the Scots were so far from being overcome that they remained on the south of the Tweed, and continued, all through the following winter, their career of rapine on English territory, with no-one to dare oppose them. By the Treaty of Durham, signed in April, 1139, the border between Scotland and England was brought down to the Tees, only the castles of Bamborough and Newcastle being retained by Stephen.

'A murderous plague to the whole of Scotland'.

RENFREW.

(1164.)

WHEN those bold sea-rovers, the Vikings, set out on their career of slaughter and pillage, the shores of the British Isles were among the first places to suffer from the swords and the torches of the Norsemen. Scotland was but a short way from the coast of Norway. The narrow sea that lay between was an easy passage for the stout war galleys of the raiders, driven by powerful sweeps and manned by crews who cared not a jot for wave or gale.

At first the Viking attacks were no more than sudden raids. The galleys were run on to some likely strip of beach; the warriors landed and spread rapidly over the countryside, burning the homesteads, slaying every man who dared await their coming, and collecting all the booty they could conveniently carry off. Then they made their way back to their ships, laden with spoil; and, before any opposition could be organised, they were safely on the high seas again, giving praise to Odin, and hasting to the feast and the flowing mead that would celebrate their valour.

Emboldened by repeated success, they became more daring. Larger fleets took the sea, greater numbers of warriors embarked under the Raven flag, and their raids spread over a greater stretch of seaboard and penetrated further into the ravaged country until, in course of time, they became actual invasions. Scottish islands were seized and held by the Norsemen, and even large portions of the mainland passed into their hands. There they maintained themselves, and from these lairs they launched their attacks on the surrounding country until they became a murderous plague to the whole of Scotland.

The islands of the Hebrides were their main stronghold. There the long galleys lurked in the creeks and sea lochs, ready to dart forth when the chance of a prey might appear. The native population was driven from its possessions or reduced to servitude, and the islands became the undisputed property of the Norsemen, whose chiefs admitted only the most vague allegiance to the Scottish kings. Indeed, in time they came to be so confident in their strength that they were prepared to dispute even the throne of Scotland with its rightful occupants. Their High Chief proclaimed himself the Lord of the Isles, and had at his command an army and a fleet such as many a monarch of the time could not boast of. With the help of his kinsmen from the Baltic, the Orkneys and the north of Ireland, he could put in the field a force that might well hope to win for him a kingdom, as had happened, indeed, once with a countryman of his in England.

The Norsemen of the isles chose the Hebrides as their domain not because of any wealth that might be got there, but solely on account of the security for their ships which they found in the narrow lochs and inlets, and in the protection which the encircling water gave them from attack by the Scots, who had no great aptitude for seafaring or sea-fighting. As skilled mariners, with islands for their strongholds, they had a tremendous advantage not enjoyed by those of their kinsmen who had forcibly settled themselves on the mainland.

At one time the whole of the north of Scotland beyond the Moray Firth was in the hands of "the Danes," as they are always referred to by the ancient chroniclers. Their leader, the earl of Orkney, was one of the most powerful of the Scandinavian chiefs. But, with his feet set firmly on land, the Scot was as good a man as the Viking. Better, in fact; for, by the time of Macbeth, Caithness and the surrounding territory had been completely cleared of the invaders. It was not done without a struggle. In the annals of the early kings there are constant references to wars with the Danes, culminating with the half-legendary battle of Mortlach, in which Malcolm II achieved a notable victory. But Scottish spears proved a match for Viking axes. The Norsemen were gradually driven towards the sea, and finally into it.

With the Lords of the Isles it was different. They had a secure retreat in their island fastnesses, where none dared approach them. Yet their eyes were ever on the mainland, with its cornfields, its fat cattle, its rich monasteries to spoil, and its fair women to ravish. Constantly they were crossing the water in their long, lean galleys, to plunder and outrage.

They shewed the greatest daring and resource in these exploits. No obstacle could dismay them, when their hearts were fired by greed or lust or the thirst for battle. Once, even, they set themselves to subdue the almost impregnable stronghold on Dunbarton Rock, and, after a siege of four months, they took it. Another time, they thought to ravage the rich lands of the Lennox. Sailing to the head of Loch Long, they dragged their ships across the neck of land between Arrochar and Tarbet, then launched them on Loch Lomond, and had the whole countryside at their mercy.

Fierce fighters they were, too, those Norsemen, men who knew neither fear nor mercy. Their joy was in the sight of blood. The titles they chose for themselves, or had bestowed on them, bear eloquent testimony to their ruthless rage in war! One has come down in history by the name of "Eric of the Red Axe." Another Eric rejoiced in the title of the "Cleaver of Skulls." And once there was a "Brainspiller."

For centuries the western Vikings were a constant terror to the Scots and a menace to the Scottish throne. It was in vain that successive kings strove to take measure for the protection of their subjects. In Scotland there was no standing force of trained fighters. An army had to be raised afresh each time there was need of one, a slow and ineffective business, and the soldiers were armed only with such weapons as they themselves might happen to possess. Once they were in the field they fought well; but the difficulty was to get them there. Seldom could that be done before the raiders had gone off with their plunder, leaving only mourning women and smoking ruins to tell where they had been.

The first king to conceive a useful plan of defence was David I. He had spent a great part of his youth at the English court, and there learned the value of the trained force of almost professional warriors which the feudal system gave to the Norman kings. He decided to introduce the system into his own realm.

From England he brought Norman knights whose acquaintance he had made there and whose valour in battle he felt that he could trust. They were given rich domains in Scotland, in return for which they became vassals of the king, and pledged themselves to maintain, for his support in time of need, a body of armed and disciplined men well exercised in the conduct of war.

Most of them were established in the west, around the Firth of Clyde, in Ayrshire, Lanarkshire and Renfrewshire, the district particularly exposed to the ravages of the Norsemen. They built themselves powerful castles, and trained their followers in the use of arms.

One of these noble immigrants was Walter Fitz Alan, a Breton knight from Shropshire. He was made High Steward of Scotland, and received lands in Renfrewshire and Ayrshire. His principal stronghold he built at Dundonald. Another of his castles was at Renfrew.

The High Chief of the Isles at this time was a somewhat mysterious figure in history. His name was Somerled, and he was married to the daughter of King Olave of Man, but beyond those facts little is known of him, although it is to him that almost every chief of an island clan to-day claims to be able to trace back his ancestry.

Somerled admitted some slight form of allegiance to

the Norse kingdom of Man; but in his own territory he
was to all intents an independent sovereign. His
relations with the king of Scots were at no time those of
subject and ruler. He seems to have been almost
constantly at variance with the king, Malcolm IV.

In the year 1164, the Lord of the Isles suddenly
determined on a bold adventure. He would be done
with petty raids and forays, and would stake his all on a
desperate attempt to overthrow the king of Scots and
seize the kingdom for himself. He was a man of no
mean ambition.

Collecting an army of his own adherents, reinforced
by fighting men from Man and the north of Ireland,
he embarked on his enterprise. With a fleet of a hundred
and sixty galleys, he burst into the Firth of Clyde and
sailed defiantly up the river. At Renfrew he landed
without opposition, and began to march southward,
reaching shortly the little hill called the Knock, midway
between Renfrew and Paisley.

What happened there has been the subject of much
learned argument, for it is shrouded in one of the hazes
of Scottish history. Some would have it that treachery
came into play and that Somerled was murdered by his
own page, his army then being thrown into confusion by
the loss of their leader. Others advance different theories
to account for an astounding fact, which perhaps valour
and discipline are sufficient to explain.

The men of the High Steward came on the invaders at
the Knock. There was but a little band of them compared to the Viking host; but they had hearts as stout
as the spears they held, and they knew well how to use
their weapons to the most deadly purpose.

With no thought of fear or of defeat, the Scots threw
themselves on the Norsemen, and the battle was over
ere it had well begun. Somerled was slain; his son fell
by his side; and soon the proud array which he had led
from the Clyde was streaming, a broken mob, in panic-
stricken flight, back to the river, to seek refuge in their

ships. The Scots were hard on their heels, and the pursuit was a bloody one. Only a remnant of the invading army escaped and won back to the Isles.

Not for many a year did the Islesmen forget that day at Renfrew, or dare again to set foot in war on the territory of the king of Scots.

200 Norwegian ships set sail for Scotland — and war!

LARGS.

(*2nd October*, 1263.)

AFTER the victory at Renfrew, the Scots felt that they were free from all peril from their Scandinavian neighbours in the west. A threat that had seemed to hold the gravest danger for them had been warded off with almost miraculous ease. They now feared nothing that the Norsemen might do. What feudal discipline had once achieved would be done again if ever the occasion should arise.

Yet there was not peace between the two races. Despite the crushing defeat that had been inflicted on their arms by the Steward's men, the Vikings held fast to their possessions in the Isles and in Argyll, although many efforts were made to dislodge them, or, at least, to compel them to own fealty to the crown of Scotland. Argyll was made a Scottish shire, but it was only in name. The sheriff dared not put his foot within his province, for the only allegiance the chiefs there would accept was a slender one to either the king of Man or the king of Norway. In actual fact they were completely independent of both, and were petty kings themselves in their own domains.

Both William the Lion and his successor Alexander II made several ineffective attempts to enforce Scottish sovereignty in Argyll and the Hebrides. It was during one such expedition that Alexander died at Kerrera.

It was a deeper reason than mere desire for extension of their power and territory that prompted the Scottish kings to reduce these Norsemen to vassalage. The lands in dispute were really the cradle of the Scottish race, which had had its origin in the west. The Lothians

24

and the Borderlands were comparatively late acquisitions. It was regarded, then, as intolerable and a standing rebuke to the majesty of Scotland that men of an alien breed should occupy the sacred soil which had been the nucleus of the kingdom.

The king of Norway was brought into the dispute. He regarded Argyll and the Hebrides as forming part of his dominions, although he knew well that he could exercise not a scrap of authority there. It was a matter of principle with him. The men who occupied these areas were of the blood of his people, and must therefore be, in name at least, his subjects. He had to look, also, beyond the western isles. If they should pass under the sceptre of Scotland, what then was likely to happen to the other islands adjacent to that kingdom, the Orkneys and Shetlands, over which his rule was undisputed? These latter were rich possessions; their people were wealthy and powerful. On no account could they be suffered to be lost.

Alexander III sought to discuss the matter in peaceful fashion. He sent ambassadors to Norway, to consult with King Haco as to how terms might be arranged. But the Norwegian king had heard tales that frightened him, tales of attacks by the Scots on the Islesmen, adorned with a wealth of more than barbaric cruelty, and he trembled for the safety of his faithful Jarl of Orkney. He sent Alexander's messengers home again, having told them that he meant to defend his rights to the utmost of his power. His subsequent invasion of Scotland was the result of this resolution. It was prompted more by a spirit of self-protection than by one of offence and thirst for conquest.

Having decided on an armed expedition to Scotland, in defence, as he thought, of his countrymen there, Haco, in the winter of 1262, took steps to call a muster of all the fighting men in his realm who owed him service. He was readily obeyed, and in the following summer a mighty fleet of over two hundred ships assembled at

Bergen, manned by the finest seamen and the bravest warriors in Norway, all eager to be led against the foe.

The king's son, Magnus, wished to be given command of the armada, to relieve his father of the labour and care of such a task. The old man was far stricken in age; he had reigned for six and forty years; but his heart was as young as ever it had been, and he would trust no one but himself with the responsibility of maintaining the fair name of Norway on the battlefield. He appointed his son to be regent of the kingdom, and himself took command of the fleet. In July, 1263, the Norse ships set sail for the Orkneys.

To form a proper estimate of Haco's force it is necessary to realise that the Norwegian ships of his time were by no means the insignificant vessels that one may be tempted to suppose. Admirably adapted to their purpose by a combination of strength and lightness, they were clinker-built ships, with the planks carefully fitted together and mortised into the frame. They had square sails, but depended for their movement mainly on their long sweeps, each pulled by two or three men. Some of them had as many as thirty oars. As to size, a favourite vessel, the *Long Serpent*, described with pride in the sagas, must have had a length of over a hundred feet. Many of the galleys were richly ornamented with gilded carving, and bore on their bows or their sails the devices which, in the primitive heraldry of the period, were the badges of the chieftains who commanded them.

Haco's fleet spent some days at Ronaldsvo, where the crews were feasted by their countrymen of the Orkneys. There an awful sign appeared which might well have daunted them. The sun went out of the sky, and darkness spread over the face of the heavens. But even an eclipse, little as it can have been understood by men of an unlearned age and a superstitious race, had not the power to make Haco and his warriors turn back. They sailed on to Caithness, and then to the Western Isles.

In the Hebrides they found the chiefs in a quandary. The Islesmen were torn between two sentiments, or three in fact; sympathy with the king of Norway, fear of the king of Scots, and dislike for kings in general. The Norwegians were of their own kindred, but the Scots were their near neighbours. Which could· most safely be supported and which offended? And what would be the effect on the liberties of the isles of the victory of either of them?

Where Haco had looked to find loyal allies and a considerable accession to his strength, he met only with guarded sympathy and not too warm hospitality. At Skye, however, he was joined by his son-in-law, Magnus, king of Man, with some ships and men.

As the fleet made its way down the west coast of Scotland, there were frequent landings and raids on the scattered and unprotected homesteads and villages. The natives, taken mostly by surprise, were quite un-prepared to offer any resistance to the invaders. The most notable of these incursions were made by Magnus of Man. Moving with a squadron of some sixty ships, in advance of the rest of the fleet, he sailed to the head of Loch Long. There he learned that Loch Lomond was little more than a couple of miles away, across an isthmus that presented no very great natural obstacles; so he had several of his galleys landed and dragged on rollers from the sea to the great inland lake, where they were launched again, and proceeded to strike terror into the astonished natives. In the Lennox they found a rich countryside and spoil in abundance to reward their daring enterprise.

Meanwhile Haco, with the main body of his fleet, swept round the long peninsula of Kintyre, and anchored his ships in the firth of Clyde, between Arran and the Ayrshire coast. Then, instead of making an immediate attack, as might have been expected of a man skilled in

war, he entered into negotiations with the leading
Scots of the district.   Who those were has not been
recorded, but it may be taken as certain that they had
no authority from the king to enter into any agreement
that entailed the bartering away of part of his kingdom.

Yet the Norwegian annalists state that the Scots were
willing to yield up Arran, Bute and the Cumbraes in
exchange for peace.   They may have professed to be,
but they took their own time about coming to terms.
The reason is not far to seek.   While the parleys were
dragging on, armed men were gathering in ever increasing
numbers among the hills that skirt the seaboard of
Ayrshire.   And another aid was hastening to the Scots.
Autumn and its gales were fast approaching, to harass
the invaders with the storms which beat so fiercely on the
treacherous shores of the firth.   It is surely astonishing
that the Norwegian king, the leader of so mighty a
host, allowed himself to be played with in such a
fashion.   Saint Andrew, to whom doubtless the Scots
prayed fervently, seemed to be fulfilling his promise to
them, for how else would a man like Haco, tried in war,
waste precious time in argument, when in a swift stroke
lay obviously his best hope of victory?

The storms came, and with them disaster to the
Norsemen.   Ships struck against ships, others were
driven ashore, galleys were stove in and sunk, men were
drowned, provisions began to run short and fresh supplies
were hard to come by.   Yet still Haco held his hand,
until at last he was compelled by circumstance to do
what he should have done on his first arrival, and to do
it on ground where all the advantage was against him.

Some of his galleys were stranded on the shore at
Largs, and their crews fell into a dispute with a party of
the Scots.   Words gave way to blows, and soon the
Norsemen were having the worst of it.   Groups of
their comrades landed, to come to their assistance.
but always they were overborne by the Scots who came
pouring down from the hills, until Haco was constrained

to give orders for the landing of his whole force, and a general action commenced.

There could not have been a worse arena for such a battle, from the Norse point of view. Haco would never have selected it of deliberate choice, for, as his men were landed on the narrow strip of rocky beach, they were commanded immediately by their enemies, who were posted strongly on the higher ground which runs down almost to the shore. It was impossible for them to get into any orderly formation which would give them a chance against the Scots.

Of the composition of the Scottish army we know nothing. It probably consisted mostly of armed peasantry from Ayrshire and Renfrewshire, under the command of their feudal superiors, by whom they had been given a rough training in military exercises, an army of the sort that was later to prove its worth on many a field. According to the Norse accounts, there were in the ranks of the Scots fifteen hundred men-at-arms, mounted and in mail. That such a figure might be correct is most unlikely, though doubtless the High Steward, Boyd, Montgomerie and other barons were there with bands of well-equipped retainers.

As to the leaders of the Scottish host there is little record. The king was not there. Prominence is given by the ancient chroniclers to the doughty deeds of one knight, Sir Piers Curry. He may have been the commander, although that honour is claimed by some for Alexander, the fourth High Steward. According to Bellenden, at a critical phase of the battle "Alexander Stewart of Paisley" arrived with "a bachment of fresche men," with whom he forced the invaders to give way, then pursued them with great slaughter through Cunningham.

To whomever the credit may be due, the Scots were well organised and well led. They harassed the Norsemen as they came ashore, prevented them from forming up for battle, and finally inflicted on them a crushing defeat, slaying perhaps the most of them and forcing the remainder in terrified confusion back to their ships, on which they fled as fast as sails and oars would drive them. Scottish annalists of the period claim that 25,000 Norsemen were slain. The usual patriotic exaggeration of the mediæval historian' must be allowed for.

King Haco escaped from the field of battle, but he was not destined long to survive it. Reaching the safety of the Orkneys, he was seized with a sickness there and felt that his end was at hand. After visiting the great church of St. Magnus, and doing his devotions at the shrine of its founder, he ordered the Bible and the "Lives of the Saints" to be read to him. But sainthood had little appeal for the old warrior. He dismissed the soldiers of the Church in favour of those of his country. While he lay in bed, slowly passing, he had the chronicles of the kings of Norway recited to him. And thus he died.

The king of Scots lost no time in using to its utmost the advantage which the victory at Largs had given him. He determined, firstly, to reduce to subjection the kingdom of Man, and prepared a formidable expedition for that purpose. But king Magnus did not wait to be subdued by force of arms. He submitted without a struggle, met Alexander at Dumfries, and did homage, admitting himself and his heirs the liegemen of the Scottish kings.

Those chiefs of the Western Isles who had given any countenance to Haco were made to pay dearly for their loyalty to their blood. The earl of Mar, with a strong force, was turned loose on them. Some were executed, others were fined, and all who retained their lands were compelled to yield allegiance to the Scottish throne.

Three years after the battle of Largs a formal treaty was concluded between Alexander of Scotland and the new king of Norway, in which the latter ruler abandoned all claim to suzerainty over Man and the Hebrides, news that the young queen had died on her voyage from Norway.

The throne of Scotland was empty once more, and a plethora of claimants to it arose, no fewer in the end than thirteen of them. Civil war seemed imminent. There was but one way to avoid it, and that was taken, with the consent of all parties involved. It was obvious that the only peaceful solution of the difficulty lay in the appointment of an arbiter to decide among the claims of the competitors. Edward of England was chosen for the office. He accepted it, on condition that every one of the claimants would admit the right of the English throne to suzerainty over Scotland. This they did, each and all of them. There is no need to search far for the motive which inspired them to this treachery to their country.

Edward gave his ruling, in all fairness, in favour of John de Balliol, who, according to modern ideas of primogeniture, had undoubtedly a prior claim to that of his nearest rival, Bruce.

The judgement was accepted. Balliol did homage to Edward, and became king of Scots. His fealty was soon to be put to the test.

Edward was contemplating an invasion of France. He summoned Balliol to attend him with his feudal following. Then Balliol performed the one courageous act of his life. He renounced his homage, defied the English king, and declared his intention of entering into an offensive and defensive alliance with France.

Instantly the two countries were ablaze. Armies were raised. Edward's invaded Scotland, and the Scots prepared to meet him. At Dunbar the battle took place. The Scots were defeated; and Edward proceeded to annex their country and set garrisons of his men in every quarter of it.

John Balliol, with no further heart for kingship, voluntarily gave up his crown, and the earl of Surrey was appointed Guardian of the kingdom, with other Englishmen as Treasurer and Justiciar. Edward, however, acted, according to his lights, with the strictest justice, far beyond the usual practice of his age. Apart from his unwarranted seizure of suzerainty, there is little complaint to lay against him. He indulged in no revenge in the form of executions; he treated his captives generously; and his occupation of the strongholds of Scotland was essential to his policy. If his lieutenants acted with savagery, as so many of them doubtless did, it was not by his instruction.

The flame of patriotism seemed to be completely extinguished in the breasts of the Scottish nobles of the higher ranks. The majority of them owned rich estates in England, and, afraid to risk the loss of these, they submitted humbly to the claims of the English king. It was only among lesser men that any show of spirit was to be found, men whose wealth, if they had any, lay entirely in Scotland. Of these the most prominent was a young man named William Wallace, then little more than a youth, his age being probably about twenty-four.

He was the second son of Sir Malcolm Wallace, a simple knight whose modest holding was at Elderslie, near Paisley. The family was an ancient one; but it had never been either rich or powerful.

Wallace had two main characteristics, an iron frame and an indomitable spirit. He was insensible of fatigue, and, when he had formed a resolution, could not be made to alter it by any power on earth. In temper he was hasty and passionate, ever ready to meet an offence with a blow. From his earliest years he had nourished an intense hatred of the English. The sight of them now, lording it in high-handed insolence throughout the length of Scotland, roused in him a furious rage. He took to the hills, and gathered round him there a band of like spirits, men vowed to Scotland's freedom.

Quickly the little army grew, and soon it began to make its presence in the country felt. Detached parties fall. As Treasurer he had been a cruel extortionist; but he was made to pay for every groat he had wrung from his victims. His skin was torn from his body and cut into pieces as trophies of vengeance.

Twenge, with his nephew by his side, managed to cut his way through the press of his enemies and to rejoin Surrey on the southern bank of the river. He was one of the few Englishmen to escape the awful carnage at the foot of the Abbey Craig. There was no quarter given by the Scots that day. No prisoners were taken. Their only thought was to kill, for the richest ransom was not to be compared with the fierce joy of revenge.

A helpless spectator of the slaughter of the flower of his army, Surrey stood on his side of the river, watching the flash of the Scottish blades as they mowed through English flesh, hearing the unheeded cries for mercy of his vanquished followers. Then a sudden panic seized him.

He might have defended the passage of the river by the Scots. But he gave up all for lost. Abandoning his baggage to the victors, he hurriedly assembled those of his troops who had the good fortune not to have crossed the river, and fled precipitately southward, not to halt till the safety of Berwick was reached.

On the trampled ground between the Forth and the Abbey Craig he left twenty thousand of his countrymen lying in their blood.

On the side of the Scots the only man of note to be slain was Sir Andrew Moray; and even among the lesser men there were few who perished, for such was the terror with which the English were stricken that they made little attempt even to defend themselves.

Day when the dreams of Wallace died for ever

FALKIRK (I).

(22nd July, 1298.)

THE inevitable result of the victory at Stirling was a revival of the spirit of independence throughout the length of Scotland. Men of every degree had their faith in their country restored, and, taking courage at last, hastened to declare their adherence to the party of liberty. Among those who now threw in their lot with the patriots were the High Steward and the earl of Lennox who, as vassals of Edward for their English estates, had been with Surrey's army. They had stood aside during the fighting at the bridge, though they were apparently in secret treaty with Wallace; but, when the English retreat commenced, they threw off all pretence and led their men in the pursuit and plunder of the flying host. From the absence of their names from the list of Scottish nobles summoned, soon after the battle, to bring their vassals to Edward's support, we may perhaps safely assume that the earls of Carrick (Bruce), Caithness, Mar, Atholl and Ross had also attached themselves to the winning side.

The conduct of the majority of the Scots nobility during the War of Independence is rather difficult to estimate. They were constantly changing their allegiance, swearing fealty to England and retracting their vows again. Too much importance must not be attached to the matter of oaths in their connection. They were taken with what were known as mental reservations, and no mediæval knight believed that his honour was in the least way sullied by the breaking of an oath into which he considered he had been forced. To save his life or his estates, he would swear anything, and retract his

40

most solemn promises whenever it was to be to his benefit to do so. It was the custom of the period, practised by some of the most highly esteemed personages in history.

Scottish nobles swore fealty to the English king because in most cases they were also English landlords. They did it the more readily from the fact that few of them deeply felt their Scottish nationality. They were incomers, most of them, chiefly Normans, who had acquired estates in Scotland. Their families had not been long enough in the country for them to feel that they belonged to it. In Scotland, as elsewhere, the feudal system had broken down the old bonds of race. The only loyalties that a man felt he owed were to his feudal superior and to himself, principally to himself.

There were exceptions, of course. The Douglases were ever Scottish, in fair season and in foul. One will look in vain for the name of James of Douglas on the "Ragman's Roll," which, with the solitary other exception of William Wallace, contains the seal or the signature of every person associated later with the liberation of Scotland. The two Andrew Morays of Bothwell, father and son, were the constant supporters of Wallace, and the High Steward never wavered in his devotion to Bruce. For the most part, however, it was only the common people and the lesser barons who fully realised that they were Scots.

The battle of Stirling Bridge was followed, within a very short time by the surrender to Wallace of the castles of Dundee, Roxburgh and Edinburgh, and soon not a fortress in Scotland remained in English hands.

Wallace was appointed regent. He refused to act alone, and took the young Sir Andrew Moray as his colleague. Between them they set afoot the most energetic measures for the firm establishment of Scottish independence.

Every barony, burgh and village was required to furnish a levy of so many fighting men, between the ages

of sixteen and sixty; and to expedite the process of
conscription, which began too slowly for Wallace's taste,
a gibbet was erected in every district for the disposal
of any who might hesitate to answer the call.   This
method of recruiting was entirely successful.   Soon the
two regents had under their command such an army
as Scotland never before had known.

The question of how these troops might best be
employed did not give Wallace a moment's concern.
There was only one fit occupation for them, the immediate invasion of England, not with any thought of
conquest, but on the principle that in attack lay the
best method of defence.   When England had had a
taste of the sorrows of war she might be the more ready to
come to peace.

The English garrison was driven out of Berwick; then
Northumbria was invaded.   The Scots took full toll
for all their own losses, burning and plundering on every
hand.   "At this time," laments piteously the English
historian Hemingford, "the praise of God was unheard
in any church and monastery through the whole country
from Newcastle to the gates of Carlisle; for the monks
and priests, who were ministers of the Lord, fled, with
the whole people, from the face of the enemy; nor was
there any to oppose them, except that now and then a
few English, who belonged to the castle of Alnwick,
and other strengths, ventured from their safeholds and
slew some stragglers.   But these were slight successes,
and the Scots roved over the country from the feast of
St. Luke to St. Martin's Day, inflicting upon it all the
miseries of unrestrained rapine and bloodshed."

The tables had been turned in good earnest.   For a
month the Scots plundered and slew in Northumbria to
their hearts' content, with no man to dare to oppose them.
Then Wallace decided that the stronghold of Carlisle must
be reduced.   The garrison there, however, was found to
be both numerous and determined, and a severe winter
had set in; so, contenting himself with a final ravaging

behind the walls of spears. The slingers, too, were cutting gaps in the Scottish line. They had abundance of ammunition lying ready at their feet, and they used it to deadly purpose. All the time the men-at-arms, urged on by the fiery knights who led them, were making desperate efforts with sword and lance to hew their way to victory.

The end came suddenly. The horsemen of the Scots were gone; the bowmen were dead; only the men behind the spears remained. And among those last Edward's archers and slingers wrought havoc now. First in one schiltron, then in another, an opening was cut for the English cavalry to pass through.

Further resistance was not possible. The day had been lost and won.

With only a remnant of his army left around him, Wallace fought his way to the shelter of a near-by wood. From there they retreated to Stirling, and, unable to hold the town, set it ablaze before they retired to the security of the hills.

Edward gained little from his victory. He ravaged Fife and some of the southern counties, where there was scanty booty to reward him. Then he went home. And he was scarce across the Border before he got news that the Scots were in the field again.

To Wallace, Falkirk meant the end of all his hopes. His wonderful power over his countrymen was shattered. Other leaders took his place.

He went on a fruitless errand to the Continent, to seek for Scotland the aid of the pope and the king of France. Neither potentate had much interest in the little kingdom in the north, though the former did write an admonition to Edward, reminding him that Scotland was a free nation.

When Wallace came home it was to be betrayed, and to go to his mock trial and murder at Westminster, the darkest stain on the record of Edward of England, who elsewhere had shewn himself not only a great man but

a generous.   Yet the very fact that Edward should have
consented to stoop to such a crime, to rid himself of an
adversary, is perhaps the greatest tribute that could
have been paid to the military and political genius of
William Wallace.

MÉTHVEN (19th June, 1306).—When Robert the Bruce
had definitely rebelled against the king of England,
Edward sent a force under Aymer de Valence, earl of
Pembroke, to reduce him to subjection.   At Methven,
in Perthshire, Bruce's small band was overwhelmed,
only a handful being left to accompany the king in his
flight to the western Highlands.

MELDRUM (22nd May, 1308).—Bruce's first victory
over his enemies in a pitched battle.   With seven hundred
men he overcame a superior force, under the earl of
Buchan, at Old Meldrum on the Don.   This victory
marked the turn of the tide of his fortunes.

A crucifix for the men offering their lives to a sacred cause — liberty!

BANNOCKBURN.

(24th June, 1314.)

ONE of the most absorbing problems in the whole field of Scottish history is to be found in a study of the character of Robert the Bruce, the Norman knight who spent his youth at the court of Edward of England and in manhood became the liberator of Scotland. To what extent was he actuated by devotion to the country of his birth, and how far were his great deeds prompted mainly by the fact that he was a claimant, and in his own opinion the nearest heir to the Scottish throne.

When Alexander II was still childless, it was necessary for him, under the ancient Tanist law of Scotland, to name one of the royal line as his successor. He chose Robert de Bruce, a descendant of David I, and grandfather of the future king. To him all the barons and clerics present at the meeting of the Great Council took an oath of fealty. This was in 1238.

On the death, more than fifty years later, of Alexander III, Bruce immediately put forward his claim to the throne and secured a number of adherents among the nobility. Of the thirteen competitors adjudicated on by the king of England in 1292, he was the only one with a claim in any way to be compared with that of John Balliol.

Balliol was the grandson of the eldest daughter of David, earl of Huntingdon, grandson of David I. Bruce was the son of the earl's second daughter. According to modern ideas of succession, Balliol had undoubtedly the better case. Many of his contemporaries thought otherwise, however; and, if Bruce had not been a very

49

old man, it is unlikely that he would have submitted
tamely to Edward's decision.

His son had no thought of royal honours, but remained
all his life a trusted servant of the English king. The
grandson, however, was a man of different mettle.
Through his mother he was earl of Carrick, a greater
noble than his father, the lord of Annandale. He
was of powerful mould, both of body and mind, impatient
of opposition, and fired all his life by ambition. At
the back of his mind there was constantly the idea of a
throne. He had much to lose by rebellion against
English authority, but he had much more to gain.

The early years of the Scottish war of independence
saw Bruce playing an ignoble part, one time in arms with
Wallace, the next in the service of England. He was
with the Scottish army at Irvine. When it was dispersed,
he hastened to make his peace with Edward. Wallace's
victory at Stirling brought him back to the Scottish
side. After Falkirk he was glad to renew his homage
to England.

It is not a very creditable story. But allowance must
be made for the morality of the time, when few men
considered that an oath bound them for longer than
was convenient. The bishops of St. Andrews and Glasgow took more oaths to Edward than Bruce did, and
broke them as readily.

There is much obscurity about the history of Bruce
before he finally declared himself in 1306, but we have
occasional glimpses of him which show that, even
during the period when he is popularly supposed to have
been loyally serving England, he was working and
plotting for the day when he might take the field at the
head of a Scottish army. Within a month of the battle
of Falkirk, he was present at a meeting of Scottish
nobles in Selkirk Forest, where plans were made for
continuing the struggle against English oppression.
Later he became one of the Guardians of Scotland, with
Comyn and the bishop of St. Andrews as his colleagues;

jectured, the only definite information, in all the records, being that it was roughly about one-third the strength of Edward's. That accounts for the usual estimate of 30,000. A more probable figure would be 15,000.

When his scouts brought him word of the English approach, Bruce set about preparing to meet them. He took up his position in the New Park, thus commanding both the routes by which it was possible for Edward to advance on Stirling. Between him and his enemies ran the Bannock burn, a little winding stream which flows east, then north-east, to join the Forth about two miles east of Stirling.

There were natural advantages in this position. The burn itself was not a formidable obstacle; but between it and the Scottish line there lay two morasses, now disappeared, named Milton Bog and Halbert's Bog. If they should attempt to pass over these, the heavy English cavalry would for a certainty be foundered.

Then there were the famous pits, the feature of Bannockburn that every schoolboy knows. They were holes dug between the two bogs and in the more solid ground on their flanks. In them, concealed by sods, were sharpened stakes, whose purpose was to damage the legs of such horses as might stumble into the traps. Edward's cavalry was a numerous and well accoutred force. It was essential for Bruce to take every step possible to impede its movements.

Behind the bogs and the pits lay the main body of the Scots. The more open ground on their left, between the Park and the Forth, was guarded by a mobile detachment under Randolph. The cavalry, sadly few in number, were on the right, commanded by Sir Robert Keith. There were only five hundred lances of them, all told.

Such was the position of the Scots when, on the afternoon of Sunday, 23rd June, the English army arrived on the south side of the Bannock. The day was stiflingly warm, the men were exhausted by their march in the sun from Falkirk, and Edward decided to postpone his attack until the morrow. He thought, however, that he saw a way by which, in the meantime, the castle might at least technically be relieved before the expiry of the year of grace.

A squadron of heavy cavalry, three hundred strong, under the command of Sir Robert de Clifford, was sent to make its way round the left flank of the Scots, and establish communication with the castle. The horsemen were completely confident of success. What was there to deny it to them? Only Randolph's five hundred pikemen.

For men on foot to dare to dispute the advance of a strong body of mailed cavalry was a thing unknown in war. Only by a miracle could they survive the reckless venture. That day the miracle happened. Randolph's men set themselves in the path of Clifford's squadron, and boldly attacked the armoured horsemen with their spears, attacked them with such fearless determination that, before Douglas arrived with reinforcements, the English had first wavered and then fled, leaving many of their best knights either dead on the field or prisoners in the hands of the Scots.

About this same time, another event was happening, one of the most famous in Scottish story. The earl of Gloucester, with the English advance guard, had pressed forward from the main body, his young knights, many of them but new-made as was the custom before a battle, all eager for the fray. Bruce, thinking an attack was imminent, was riding along the front of his line, mounted only on a light palfrey. An English knight, Sir Henry de Bohun, recognised the king by the gold circlet on his helmet, and spurred forward to have the glory of winning the battle with his own hand by throwing the Scots into despair by the death of their leader. He couched his lance and rode straight at the king, who, turning his horse quickly aside, avoided the blow, and, rising in his stirrups, dealt de Bohun such a blow with his battle-axe that the Englishman's head was cleft to

BATTLE OF BANNOCKBURN
1314

A A Positions on June 23rd
B B Positions on June 24th

the chin. Then a party of the Scots leaped forward, and drove Gloucester's vanguard unresistingly back to their own line.

The Scots had drawn first blood, an omen that set them in high fettle and put doubts into the hearts of their opponents.

During the night, King Edward made some change in the position he had chosen for the battle. What that amounted to has been keenly argued, but need not be discussed at the moment.

With the first light of day both armies were astir. The Scots had mass said in front of their line, as befitted men who were offering their lives to the sacred cause of liberty. Then the abbot of Inchaffray passed from division to division of them, holding a crucifix before their eyes, and as he passed they all knelt down.

Edward saw them. "They ask mercy!" he cried exultantly.

"They do," said old Ingelram de Umfraville, "but not of you. These men will win all or die."

The English had crossed the Bannock, and were drawn up in nine divisions, the foremost commanded by the earl of Gloucester. The first line of the Scots consisted of three "schiltrons" of spearmen, commanded by Edward Bruce, Randolph and Douglas; the king was with the reserve, the Highlanders and Islesmen and the men of his own Carrick.

The battle began with a desperate charge by Gloucester's cavalry against the division of Edward Bruce. It broke like a wave on the solid wall of spears, rallied and charged again and again, but always to be driven back in confusion. Gloucester was slain, and many a gallant knight by his side.

Another English division attacked Randolph, with no more success than the first. Douglas moved forward to Randolph's support, and the battle became general.

The English archers and slingers came into the fight, and looked as if they might turn the fortunes of the day, for they sorely harassed the schiltron of Edward Bruce. But Keith and his horsemen knew how to deal with them. They were scattered, and driven from the field, to return no more.

The English king had chosen his position badly. It had too narrow a front, so that he could make no effective use of the greater part of his troops, and could not contrive to get at the Scottish flanks. As his broken divisions fell back, the situation became even worse. Men were crowded helplessly together, unable to strike a blow.

Gradually the Scots began to press forward, breaking the ranks of their enemies, and wielding their pikes to right good purpose on the men and horses that opposed them. At the same time the Scottish bowmen came into action. They "waxed hardy, and shot eagerly among the horsemen." Pressed closely together in a confused mass of footmen and cavalry, the English could neither advance nor retire nor move to either flank. They were easy victims for the spears and swords and arrows of the Scots, who, flushed with the consciousness of victory, turned what had begun as a battle into a massacre.

A few of the English managed to escape from the field. Of the others, the fortunate ones were able to purchase their lives with surrender; the remainder, an untold multitude, were slain.

Among the English dead were twenty-one barons, including the earl of Gloucester, de Clifford, and de Mauley, the Marshall of England, and according to one chronicler, seven hundred gentlemen of coat-armour. The prisoners taken by the Scots included twenty-two barons and sixty knights, the earls of Hereford and Angus among them.

King Edward himself but narrowly escaped. His attendant, Sir Giles de Argentine, told him that the day was lost and that he must look to his safety. "For myself," said the gallant knight, "I am not used to flee, nor will I do so now. I commend you to God." Then he set spurs in his horse, and plunged into the thick of

Edward Bruce's column, where he got the death which he preferred to dishonour.

Edward galloped to the castle, and demanded admittance and shelter there. But de Mowbray bade him speed on his way, else he would assuredly fall into the hands of Bruce, as the castle must now do. So he fled to Dunbar, closely pursued by Douglas.

Such, briefly, was the battle fought on the 24th of June, 1314. But where was it fought? If there is one thing certain about Bannockburn it is this, that it did not occur at the place popularly associated with it. For centuries it has been assumed that the main battle took place on the same ground as the skirmishing of the previous day, the New Park and the neighbourhood of the Borestone. All the evidence is against that. The main cause of the discomfiture of the English was that they were hemmed in. All the chroniclers are agreed on that. But there was nothing to hem them in on the supposed battlefield. The bogs and caltrops may have hindered their advance, but there were no obstacles on their flanks, and nothing to prevent their retiring if they wished.

Even more convincing evidence is to be found in the flight of Edward by way of Stirling Castle. If the battle was fought near the Borestone, he must have made his road to the castle through the ranks of his victorious enemies!

Recent students of the problem have come to the conclusion that on the Sunday night Edward moved his troops about two miles down the Bannock, and crossed that stream a little above its entry into the Forth. The battle would then be fought on the ground between the Bannock and the link of the Forth which approaches Stirling, ground which is in keeping with all the known facts of the engagement. The English army would have water on three sides of it, and only a narrow front facing the Scots. And Edward's flight to the south would take him directly past Stirling Castle.

Barbour states that the fight was "doune in the kers." The name still survives. There are Kerse Mill and Springkerse, north-east of the village of Bannockburn on the other side of the railway, and not far from the mouth of the burn. There, in all possibility, was the scene of the battle.

DUNDALK (October, 1318).—Edward Bruce, in the words of Barbour, "found Scotland too small for himself and his brother." Deciding to win a kingdom, as Robert had done, he landed at Carrickfergus in May, 1315, with an army of 6000 men, and set himself to conquer Ireland, then in English hands. He was so successful that within a year he was crowned king. For two years he maintained his position; then, with characteristic rashness, and against the advice of all his subordinate leaders, he engaged in a needless battle in which all the odds were against him, and was defeated and slain by the English at Dundalk.

MYTTON (20th September, 1319).—In 1318 Bruce captured Berwick, one of the greatest blows he had dealt to England. An English army came in the following year and laid siege to the town. To relieve the pressure on Berwick, Douglas and Randolph led a force into Yorkshire. They were met, at Mytton-on Swale, by an assembly of hastily raised levies under the archbishop of York, who hoped probably to repeat the achievement of his predecessor, Thurstan, at Northallerton. The Scots were completely victorious. Among the slain Englishmen were so many priests and monks that the battle came to be known mockingly by the Scots as "the Chapter of Mytton."

BYLAND (14th October, 1322).—Bannockburn was not Bruce's last encounter with the second Edward of England. Eight years later, in October, 1322, he defeated him again, as heavily and almost as bloodily, in the little remembered battle of Byland.

Edward had invaded Scotland, and penetrated to

Edinburgh, but had to fall back before the Scottish army.

Bruce pursued him into Yorkshire, and came up on him there. The English were in a strong position on a ridge between Byland and Rievaulx; but the Scots attacked them with such courage and determination that Edward was forced to flee for his life, leaving in the hands of the victors the whole of his baggage and most of the survivors of the army. Says Sir Thomas Gray, in *Scalachronica*, "The Scots were so fierce, and their chiefs so daring, and the English so badly cowed, that it was no otherwise between them than as a hare before greyhounds."

For six years the Scots harassed Northumbria, doing mostly as they pleased, until England sued for peace, and by the Treaty of Northampton, in May, 1328, the absolute independence of Scotland was acknowledged.

DUPPLIN MOOR (12th August, 1332).—On the death of Robert the Bruce, Edward Balliol, son of King John Balliol, made a determined attempt to capture for himself the Scottish throne. With an army of 3000 men he landed in Fife. The regent Randolph prepared to meet him, but, unfortunately for Scotland, died suddenly in July, 1332. His successor was the earl of Mar, a man of no military genius. At Dupplin Moor, near Perth, Mar's army and Balliol's met. The Scots were overcome, mainly by the English archers, and defeated with tremendous loss. Then Balliol proceeded to have himself crowned at Scone as king of Scots.

ANNAN (December, 1332).—Edward Balliol's success was short-lived. The next regent chosen by the Scots was the doughty Andrew Moray of Bothwell. He reorganised the Scottish forces, and entrusted the command of them to the earl of Moray, son of Randolph, who fell on Balliol at Annan, where he took the usurper by surprise, destroyed his army, and drove him "half naked" out of the kingdom.

Death stood waiting at the top of the hill ...

HALIDON HILL.

(19th July, 1333.)

KING ROBERT THE BRUCE died in the year 1329, at
the age of fifty-five. When his strong hand had been
removed from the control of the affairs of Scotland,
the nation, within a short time, came near to losing all
that he had gained for it.

The new king was Bruce's only son, David II, the
worst and the weakest monarch that ever sat on the
Scottish throne. At the battle of Neville's Cross he
shewed that he had all the courage of his race, but that
is the solitary thing that can be said in his favour. He
had the instincts neither of a king nor of a Scot. With
no thought for the liberties or the welfare of his people,
his only concern was his own comfort and enjoyment;
so much so that, after Neville's Cross, he preferred the
luxury of an English prison to the responsibilities of
a Scottish throne.

He cannot, however, be blamed for the disasters
which marked the beginning of his reign. At his accession he was only in his eighth year. The regency was
put into the hands of Randolph, earl of Moray, the
nephew of Bruce who helped so gallantly to carry the
day at Bannockburn. It was a good choice. Randolph
was a brave soldier, an able general and a devoted Scot.
His talents were soon to be put to the test.

By the Treaty of Northampton, in 1328, one of the
terms of peace between Scotland and England was that
certain barons, known as "the Disinherited," who had
forfeited their Scottish estates on account of their
English sympathies, were to be restored to their ancestral
property. This condition had not yet been carried

63

out at the time of the death of Bruce. It was left to Randolph to do so.

A number of the nobles concerned were known still to be strongly attached to England, and were suspected to be committed to the English king, to support him in any enterprise in which he might engage against Scotland. In their case the regent definitely refused to carry out the provision of the treaty. They were enemies, who must not be allowed to gain any footing of power in the country.

The result was the sudden re-emergence on the scene of the Balliol family. John Balliol had a son named Edward, even more of an English tool than his father had been. This man was living at the court of Edward III, the ambitious young king who had succeeded the discredited and deposed Edward II, his father. He gathered around him the disinherited lords and made a descent on Fife, with a considerable army behind him.

King Edward professed that he had forbidden Balliol's plot. No one believed him. He had every reason to wish for revenge on the Scots, who had signalised his ascent of his throne by raiding the north of his kingdom, holding him at bay for a month, and making off with an immense load of plunder. It was suspected, and, as subsequent events proved, correctly, that he contemplated the subjugation of Scotland. He had inherited his grandfather's military ardour, but not his uprightness of character. The first Edward, however hardly he may have borne on Scotland, was an honest man. What he did he did openly and with the conviction that it was his duty. His grandson was a land-grabber, greedy of gain and ambitious of power for its own sake, as his exploits in France were soon to shew.

Balliol's invasion of Scotland met with speedy and surprising success. The regent, Randolph, raised an army of defence, but died suddenly before he could take the field, a deplorable loss to his country, for, with the possible exception of another and later earl of Moray, he was the greatest of the many regents who have controlled the destinies of Scotland during the frequent minorities of her kings.

Randolph was succeeded by the earl of Mar, who took command of the army and led it against Balliol. At Dupplin Moor they met. Mar was defeated and slain; Perth was taken; and in the abbey of Scone Balliol was crowned king of Scots by the earl of Fife and the bishop of Dunkeld.

The first act of the pseudo-sovereign was to acknowledge the king of England as his liege and overlord. This he did at Roxburgh in November, 1332.

He was soon to learn, however, that neither he nor his master would be tolerated by the Scots. Another regent was chosen, Sir Andrew Moray, the faithful companion of Wallace. The army was got together again and Balliol was bundled neck and crop across the Border.

Next year he came back, this time with a numerous following of English barons and their retainers. He encamped his army in front of Berwick, and set about preparing for the reduction of that fortress.

The Scots came to meet him, and suffered a disaster, in a trifling engagement, in the capture of the regent, followed shortly by another, when Sir William Douglas, "the Knight of Liddesdale," the foremost figure of his time in Scottish chivalry, was made prisoner.

Another regent was appointed, Sir Archibald Douglas, brother of the Good Sir James, who had died, fighting against the Moors in Spain, while bearing the heart of Bruce to the Holy Land.

The English king had now thrown off all disguise, and had joined Balliol in front of Berwick, which was closely invested both by sea and land.

The governor of the town was Sir Alexander Seton. The castle was commanded by the earl of March, a man suspected of dealings with the English.

The garrison was not numerous and provisions were short, but the townsmen put up a gallant defence, in which they were encouraged for a while by their success in destroying by fire a large part of the blockading English fleet. Every assault by Edward's men met with stubborn opposition from the determined citizens, and every one failed. Soon, however, it began to appear that hunger might achieve what English spears and arrows could not do.

Their supplies almost exhausted, the men of Berwick consented to an arrangement by which they agreed to surrender the town unless aid from the Scottish army arrived by a certain day. As security for their faith, hostages were given to the English, one of them the son of Seton, the governor.

When the period of grace had all but expired and help seemed past hoping for, the spirits of the garrison were suddenly revived again by the sight, one morning, of the Scottish army crossing the Tweed at the Yare-ford and approaching the town.

Though the English tried to defend every point of entry, Sir William Keith and a number of other Scottish knights succeeded in making their way into the town, and taking with them a welcome supply of provisions.

For a day and a half the Scots army remained in front of Berwick, drawn up for battle; but the English kept to their lines. So the Scots moved away again, to pass into Northumberland, bent on pillage and burning there with the idea of creating a diversion from the investment of Berwick.

Edward was not to be drawn aside from his purpose, however. He let the Scots go, and peremptorily called on the besieged town to surrender, as, he claimed, the terms of the treaty had not been complied with within the agreed-on time. The citizens replied that the entry of Keith, with his men and supplies, had fulfilled the conditions in full, and that now they were freed of their bargain. Further, they added, they had appointed Keith as their governor, and would defend the town to the last man among them.

Edward was filled with fury, and vented his rage in a dastardly act. He sent a message that, unless the town was given up at once, he would hang his hostages in front of the eyes of the garrison. His threat had no effect. It is probable that no-one believed that he meant it; but, if so, they little knew the cruel heart of Edward Plantagenet.

A scaffold was erected before the gate of the town, and there young Seton, the son of the late governor, was hanged in full view of the men who lined the walls, his father, it is said, among them.

The citizens were aghast. They besought Keith to make a new agreement with their savage enemy, and he consented to do so. A treaty was drawn up in writing, with every detail carefully stated, by which Berwick was to be surrendered, on the 19th July, unless by that date two hundred Scottish men-at-arms should have entered it by dry land.

Keith was permitted to send word of this arrangement to Douglas, the regent, who thereon decided to venture the fate of his army and his country in a pitched battle with the English.

Retiring from Northumberland, on the 18th July he led his men across the Tweed at a little distance from Berwick, and marched towards the town.

Edward accepted the challenge. He took up his position on the crest of a slope known as Halidon Hill, and awaited the oncoming of the Scots. His tactics were excellent. At the foot of the slope was a wide marsh, which no cavalry could possibly cross; while the hill itself was sufficiently steep to give considerable trouble to armoured men in the mounting of it.

The veriest tyro in war must have seen at a glance that a frontal attack on the English position would be the most reckless folly. Or so one would think. Yet the

Scottish army, with so many tried leaders and veteran soldiers in its ranks, made the desperate attempt.

At the marsh the Scottish knights had to halt when they found that their heavy chargers sank to the hocks in the bog. The horses were given over to sutlers, to be taken to the rear, and the fighting men went on on foot, struggling with difficulty across the treacherous ground, while from the hill the English bowmen rained a torrent of arrows on them. So fast and thick flew those shafts that, in one account of the fight, they are described as being like motes in a sunbeam.

Few of the attackers reached even the foot of the hill. Those who did were rallied on the lower slopes, and, with consummate gallantry, set themselves to attempt the impossible. Hampered, as so many of them were, by their heavy armour, and in the face of the showers of English arrows, they charged up the hillside and threw themselves into the midst of their foes, there to be overwhelmed by the mass of their enemies.

For the Scots, the fight at Halidon Hill was a tragic example of the price that may be exacted for reckless daring; but it was an epic of bravery. The men who won through the morass must have known well that death stood waiting them at the top of the hill. They might have thrown down their arms. But they preferred to die.

The regent was slain, and with him the earls of Ross, Lennox, Atholl, Carrick, Sutherland, and Strathearn, besides a host of lesser barons, knights and squires. So heavy, indeed, was the loss of the Scottish nobility, that, in their rejoicings, the English told themselves that their wars with the Scots were over at last, since no man was left in Scotland fit to raise an army or to command it in the field. One of them, a soldier-poet, made a song about it.

> Scots out of Berwick and out of Aberdeen,
> At the burn o' Bannock ye were far too keen.
> Many guiltless men ye slew, as was clearly seen.
> But King Edward has avenged it now, and fully too, I ween.

Was it a premonition that made him add:

Woe worth the while!
I bid you all beware of Scots, for they are full of guile.

Though Balliol and Edward divided Scotland between them as they chose, though English armies three times ravaged the country from the Tweed to the Moray Firth, the determination for independence never died in Scottish breasts. On Robert, the High Steward, son of Marjory Bruce, fell the mantle of his grandsire, and under him the War of Independence was repeated, until once more not one hostile English foot stood on Scottish soil.

NEVILLE'S CROSS (17th October, 1346).—In the interest of France, with which country England was then at war, David II led a Scottish army across the Border in 1346. At Neville's Cross, near Durham, he was defeated in a battle which must be counted as a national disaster for the Scots. They were routed by the English archers, and the king, with great numbers of his nobles, was taken prisoner.

A Duel at Daybreak then the English surrender!

OTTERBURN.

(19th August, 1388.)

FOR centuries the Borders of Scotland and England were continuously at war, whether the two kingdoms themselves happened to be at variance or not. There were constantly raids by one side and the other, and periodically a battle of greater or less degree. Neither Scot nor Englishman could feel himself safe from sudden attack, or count his life secure even in the shelter of his own home.

There was a stretch of territory along the Border, known as the Debatable Land. It was claimed by both Scots and English, and could not be said ever to belong to either. A kind of "No-man's land," to employ a more modern term, it was the scene of almost perpetual warfare; and even beyond it, for a depth of many miles into each country, no man could lie down at night with reasonable assurance that his roof would not be ablaze before the morning.

The lesser chiefs on each side of the line lived largely on the fruits of their raids into the enemy's territory, the cattle and sheep that were brought back from the foray. There is the well-known story of the laird who sat down one day to his dinner, and, lifting the cover of the dish, discovered on the plate only his own steel spurs, put there by the goodwife as a hint that the larder was empty and it was time for the laird and his men to be over the Border in the moonlight.

The greater men, the nobles, did not take part in this system of almost legitimised robbery. Their stomachs were not dependent on their swords. But they had their feuds none the less. The foremost were the Percies

70

and the Douglases, haughty Englishmen and haughty Scots.

> There never was a time on the Marche partes
> Since the Douglas and Percy met
> But 'tis marvel an the red blood run not
> As the rain does in the street.

With those two families war was a gallant game, a thing of no hatred, but only of glory and honour, yet none the less bloody a business for all that.

At times the governments of the two countries gave those fiery neighbours the pleasure of more regular warfare than mere affairs of raids and feuds. At intervals there were invasions and retaliations, in which a considerable amount of blood was spilt, but, strange to say, no very marked ill-feeling seems to have been displayed.

More than once John of Gaunt led an army into Scotland. After his second visit, when peace had been made, he was kept as an honoured, and apparently appreciated, guest at Edinburgh Castle, because, on account of the Peasants' Revolt, it was not safe for him to go home. On his next invasion, he did "as little evil as he could, for the courtesy and hospitality which he had received."

Stout old John had a nephew, however, Richard II, a man of different breed. Dissatisfied, doubtless, with his uncle's humanity, he led an army into Scotland himself, and "ravaged all things in his pride, sparing nothing, saving nothing, and having no mercy on age or on religion." He burned down the abbeys of Melrose, Dryburgh and Newbattle, but Holyrood Abbey was reluctantly spared on the intercession of Gaunt.

The Scots determined on vengeance. A meeting of the Great Council was held in Edinburgh. The king, Robert II, then an old man, was all for peace, but his lords would have none of it. They believed in the doctrine of a tooth for a tooth, and they had memories of a previous invasion of Northumbria, a glorious looting expedition, from which the Scots had returned laden with more wealth than could then have been found in the whole of Scotland.   They would go back again.

A general muster of the whole military force of the kingdom was ordered and was eagerly fulfilled.   At Yetholm, near Jedburgh, there assembled an army which is said to have amounted to forty thousand men, including twelve hundred mounted and mailed men-at-arms.   The command was given to the earl of Fife, the second son of the king.   With him he had the flower of Scottish chivalry.

The force was divided into two.   The main body, under Fife, was to march through Liddesdale towards Carlisle and the west of England.   A smaller party, not more than five thousand strong, was to make a dash for Newcastle, with the object of diverting the attention of the English from the operations of the main Scottish army.   It was commanded by the earl of Douglas, a man still young but already renowned in war.   The ablest and most doughty knights in Scotland were among his companions, the earls of March and Moray, Sir James Lindsay, Sir Alexander Ramsay, Sir John St. Clair, Sir Patrick Hepburn, Sir John Maxwell, Sir Alexander Fraser, Sir Adam Glendinning, Sir David Fleming, Sir Thomas Erskine, and many another gallant warrior, all good men and tried with sword and lance.

Douglas pushed rapidly through Northumbria, scarcely halting until he had reached the bishopric of Durham, which was his first objective.   So swift had been his advance that the English leaders had no word of it until the smoke of burning houses and villages around Durham apprised them of the presence of the Scots.   After several days of undisputed pillage the raiders made for Newcastle, behind whose walls lay the troops of the earl of Northumberland, afraid to venture forth lest Douglas's men should only be the vanguard of the great Scottish army which they knew had been raised.

Newcastle was perhaps the strongest town in the north of England.   Besides its walls, it had around it a moat sixty feet broad. With no siege machinery, Douglas could make no attempt at reducing it. Perhaps he never intended to. He was not disappointed in his expectation of a fight, however. Those were the days of some of the most fantastic exploits of chivalry.

In Newcastle was Sir Harry Percy, Harry Hotspur as he was called, the son of the earl of Northumberland, and it would have been an unheard of thing for a Percy and a Douglas to be content to glower at each other with a wall between them. They must come to blows.

Percy sent a challenge to Douglas, offering to come out of the town and meet him in single combat. The gage thus thrown was immediately taken up. Lists were arranged, and, in sight of both armies, the two champions faced each other, mounted on their mailed destriers and armed cap-a-pie.

They ran a course, and Douglas had the better of it. Having unhorsed his opponent, however, he did not avail himself of his right to despatch his enemy out of hand, as the laws of chivalry allowed him to do. He contented himself with tearing the pennon from Percy's spear and fixing it on his own lance, vowing that he would fly it from the highest tower of his castle of Dalkeith till its owner came to fetch it again.

"That, so help me God," said Hotspur, "no Douglas will ever do." And he was fain to be as good as his word. When Douglas had raised the siege and marched away towards the north, it was not long before Percy, who had discovered that the main army of the Scots was far away, was hard on his heels, with all the men he could muster. The English force is said to have amounted to six hundred cavalry and eight thousand footmen.

Douglas had made his camp at Otterburn, in Redesdale, about ten miles from Newcastle. It was on a little hill, with a marsh in front of it, and was fortified, as well as time had permitted, against the chance of a surprise attack. There he put up his tent, and in front of the door of it he stuck a lance in the ground, with Percy's pennon fluttering at the point of it.

Late on the evening of the 19th August, Hotspur arrived to keep his tryst. The sun had long set, but there was a full moon, so Percy decided to begin the action without delay.

Scarcely allowing time for his men to form for the attack, he bade them set on, which they did with right good will, hurling themselves on the Scots in an effort to snatch a sudden victory and recover the precious trophy of their leader.

But the men in the camp were too seasoned soldiers to allow themselves to be taken unawares. The cries of "A Percy! A Percy!" which suddenly broke the calm of the summer night, were answered by defiant shouts of "A Douglas! A Douglas!" The Scots had rushed to arms on the first alarm, and were prepared to give as good as they might get in the way of blows.

At first the force of superior numbers told in favour of the English. Douglas's men were borne back, yielding their ground slowly, foot by foot. But their chief, with Sir Patrick Hepburn by his side, forced his way to the front of the battle and there turned the tide, firing his men, by the force of his example, to even greater valour than was theirs by nature.

He did it at the cost of his life. When the alarm sounded, he had not waited even to don his helmet before rushing from his tent. Now, with three spear wounds in his breast, he was brought to the ground by a blow on the head from an iron mace. His followers rallied round him, beat off their enemies, and carried him to the rear.

His skull had been broken, and he was dying fast; yet still his only thought was of the outcome of the battle. Dreading lest his men might learn that he had been slain, and so lose heart for the fight, his last order was that he might be laid in a thicket of bracken, there to die unseen.

It was given to his nephew, Sir Hugh Montgomerie, his sister's son.

> My nephew good, the Douglas said,
> What recks the death of ane!
> Last night I dream'd a dreary dream,
> And I ken the day's thy ain.

> My wound is deep; I fain would sleep;
> Take thou the vanguard of the three,
> And hide me by the bracken bush
> That grows on yonder lilye lee.

> Oh, bury me by the bracken bush,
> Beneath the blooming brier;
> Let never living mortal ken
> That ere a kindly Scot lies here.

His wish was obeyed, and his men fought on, all ignorant of the loss of their gallant leader.

> The Gordons good, in English blood
> They steeped their hose and shoon;
> The Lindsays flew like fire about,
> Till all the fray was done.

All through the summer night the battle raged about the little hill by the bank of the Otterburn, with neither side able to claim the advantage till the sun had risen again.

Montgomerie was seeking for Percy, and about day-break he found him. The Scot made straight for his enemy, who was nothing loth to meet him. They closed in a duel with their heavy swords, fighting fiercely till Hotspur had his blade stricken from his grasp, and Montgomerie had him at his mercy.

> "Yield thee, O yield thee, Percy," he said,
> Or else I vow I'll lay thee low,"
> "Whom to sall I yield?" said Earl Percy,
> "Now that I see it must be so?"

> "Thou sallt not yield to lord nor loun,
> Nor yet sallt thou yield to me;
> But yield thee to the bracken bush
> That grows upon yon lilye lee."

Such is the tale of how "a dead Douglas won a fight." With the surrender of their leader, the English began to give way, and soon the Scots were everywhere the masters of the field.

Froissart, who had his account of the engagement from men who had been there, states that "of all the battles which I have made mention of in this history, this of Otterburn was the bravest and the best contested; for there was neither knight nor squire but acquitted himself nobly, doing well his duty, and fighting hand to hand without either stay or faintheartedness."

He tells us that more than eighteen hundred English men were slain in the battle. Of much more importance to the victors was the vast number of prisoners, some of them the most famous and wealthiest knights of Northumbria. Their ransoms enriched many a needy Scottish family for many a day. With the money paid for Percy, Montgomerie built his castle of Polnoon.

The body of Douglas was taken home, to be buried beside his forebears in the Abbey of Melrose. Beside it walked all the way his chaplain, a priest named Lundie, who had refused to leave him even in the press of the battle. When the wounded earl was found by Montgomerie, Lundie was standing over him, swinging a battle-axe fiercely around him, and defying any Englishman to approach his dying master. They were worthy men and stalwart, the Scottish clerics of the fourteenth century.

HOMILDON HILL (14th September, 1402).—With a Scottish army, the earl of Douglas had been ravaging the north of England. As he was making his way back to the Border, he found himself faced, at Homildon Hill, near Wooler in Northumberland, by a large force collected by "Hotspur" Percy and other Northumbrian nobles. The Scots took their position on the side of the hill, from which they attempted to make a charge on their enemies, but their ranks were so broken by the deadly accuracy of the fire of the English bowmen that they never reached their objective. They fled in confusion, leaving many prisoners in the hands of the English.

No winners or losers as 1,000 Highlanders die

HARLAW.

(24th July, 1411.)

ALTHOUGH Somerled of the Isles was slain at the battle of Renfrew, and his eldest son with him, his race was fated to disturb the peace of Scotland for centuries after, though not with Viking rovers such as had been his following. Through a succession of Celtic mothers the Norse strain in the family was gradually overborne, and they became the chiefs of a great federation of Highland clans, both in the Isles and on the mainland.

Somerled had two sons whose names have survived, Ronald, whose descendants became the Lords of the Isles, and Dougal, ancestor of the MacDougals, the Lords of Lorn.

At the beginning of the fifteenth century the Lord of the Isles was Donald, whose descent was as follows. By Margaret, daughter of King Robert II, he was the son of John, son of Angus Og, son of Angus Mor, son of Donald, son of Ronald, son of Somerled.

By his time the house of the Isles had recovered its position as practically an independent sovereignty, ruling over all the Hebrides and considerable parts of the western mainland of Scotland. The strong hand of Bruce had kept it in comparative loyalty to the Scottish throne during his reign; but, amid the disorders and civil war which disturbed the country for so many years after his death, the island chiefs had succeeded in throwing off even the pretence of allegiance.

Even at a considerably later date than the time of Donald, they looked on themselves as kings, and were acknowledged as such by other rulers, though never, of course, by the king of Scots. Sir Walter Scott refers to a deed, signed in 1461 by John of the Isles, by whom ambassadors were appointed to meet representatives of Edward IV, king of England. The conference took place, and a treaty was drawn up. It was agreed that John, his children and all his subjects should become vassals of Edward, and should assist him in subduing the kingdom of Scotland. In return John was to receive a subsidy from England, and was to have a rich share in the partition of the conquered territory.

Nothing apparently came of this precious arrangement, but it is interesting as shewing the state of the Isles at that time. There was no serious breach of the peace, however, until the beginning of the fifteenth century, during the regency of Albany, uncle of the young king James I.

When Alexander Leslie, earl of Ross, died, he left no direct heir to his title or his estates. His only daughter Euphemia had become a nun, and had made over her inheritance to her uncle, the earl of Buchan, son of Albany.

There was another claimant, however. Donald of the Isles had married Margaret Leslie, sister of the late earl, and, in virtue of his wife's claim, he maintained that he himself was now the rightful heir to the earldom. According to the custom of the time, there was much to be said for this contention; and, even if Donald had no right of inheritance, there can be little doubt that his children had.

Albany, however, would have none of it, as was only to be expected when the fortune of his own son was at stake. He rejected the claim of the Islesman, and installed the earl of Buchan in possession of the rich lands of Ross.

Donald of the Isles was not the man to accept meekly what he felt, with good enough reason, was a flagrant injustice. He gathered together his vassals, and set about the invasion of Scotland. Such an exploit presented no difficulty to him. In a short time he had collected around him ten thousand armed men, and to

transport them from the islands he had at his command
the finest fleet that could then have been found on the
British seas.

Armed with claymores and axes, and the deadly dirks
that could work such havoc, the fierce men of the Isles
poured into Ross. There was no one there who would
dare to oppose them; so the whole district fell quickly
into their hands.

Then Donald ordered a general muster at Inverness
of his own men and of levies from Ross. His plan was to
march to Aberdeen, plunder that wealthy burgh, then,
turning southwards, to seize the whole country north of
the Tay. His ambition, it would appear, was to make
himself master of all the territory in the west and north
of Scotland, creating there a Celtic kingdom, and leaving
to the king of Scots only the Lothians and the south.

To meet this dangerous threat, Albany put a Scottish
army under the command of the earl of Mar, an interesting individual with a career that was typical of those
troublesome times. He was the son of the Wolf of
Badenoch, that ferocious scion of the royal line, who had
devastated the north with fire and sword, burning
houses and churches for the sheer joy of destruction,
drenching the land in blood for the lust of slaughter.
The son had begun life as the father's able lieutenant,
and later had been his successor in evil-doing. But
there came his way the chance of greater profit in virtue.
Having forced the widowed Countess of Mar to marry
him, he took over her estates and her late husband's
title with them. Thenceforth he was one of the pillars
of chivalry, renowned throughout Europe as a very
perfect knight; and was now the foremost and most
trusted baron in Scotland.

Under the earl's banner were assembled all the knights
and squires of Mar, Angus and the Mearns, with their
feudal retainers; while the provost of Aberdeen joined
him with a considerable body of armed burgesses,
prepared to take the field in defence of hearth and home.

From Aberdeen, Mar's force marched by way of Inverurie, and at Harlaw, in Garioch, encountered the Highlanders and Islesmen, who had left, in their passage through Moray, a trail of rapine and bloodshed.

Led, under Donald, by the chiefs of MacLean and Mackintosh, the Highlanders, who had been adding recruits to their strength through the whole length of their march from Inverness, vastly outnumbered the Lowlanders. The latter, however, made up in discipline and in experience of war for what they lacked in numbers. Mar's vanguard was led by Sir James Scrymgeour, the hereditary Standard-Bearer of Scotland. The earl himself commanded the main body, in whose ranks were the Irvings, the Maules, the Morays, the Straitons, the Leslies, the Stirlings and the Lovels, under their chiefs, all good men and true, well-armed and inured to war, and all convinced that one mailed man-at-arms was a match for several half-naked Highland savages. The douce citizens of Aberdeen can have had little experience of battlefields, but they were stout lads, prepared to give blow for blow with any caterans; and their purses were at stake, a most powerful incentive to valour.

Scarcely had the two armies come face to face, when they rushed together in a furious clash of battle, the Highlanders hacking and thrusting with their claymores, the Lowlanders advancing in a compact body with their spears levelled in front of them. Soon Mar's men had penetrated right to the heart of the press of their foes, who are said, in the records of the time, to have outnumbered them by ten to one.

Yelling the slogans of their clans, the fierce hordes of Highlanders surged around the square of knights and men-at-arms and townsmen, who stood shoulder to shoulder in the centre of the battle. Flashing in the sun, the claymores rose and fell, hewing down the foremost ranks of the Lowland men, who, too closely engaged now to ply their spears, fought desperately with sword and axe and iron mace.

Until sun-down the slaughter went steadily on. Dead men and dying lay, steeped in blood, all over the field, trodden on by the living, who refused to be dismayed by the fate of so many of their fellows, but still cut and smote and stabbed, adding ever to the heaps of the slain.

The battle of Harlaw was not lost or won; there was no flight and no pursuit. As night fell, the two forces drew gradually apart, abandoning the fight from sheer fatigue. Donald fell back on Inverurie. Mar, with those who were left to him of his men, spent the night on the battlefield, not as a token of victory, but because they were so wearied that they could do no more than lie down where they had stood.

In the morning the Highland army began to move slowly back towards its fastnesses in the west. It had not been defeated; but it had lost almost a thousand of its bravest warriors, including the chiefs of the MacLeans and the Mackintoshes, and had no more heart for the struggle.

Of the Lowlanders, more than five hundred had been slain, perhaps half of their total force. Among them were Scrymgeour, Sir Alexander Ogilvy, Sheriff of Angus, Sir Alexander Irvine of Drum, Sir Robert Maule of Panmure, Sir Thomas Murray, Sir William Abernethy of Salton, Sir Alexander Straiton of Lauriston, and most of the principal gentry of Buchan. Sir Robert Davidson, the provost of Aberdeen, and the greater part of his soldier-burgesses, went down before the claymores.

After so indecisive an engagement, Albany naturally feared that Donald of the Isles had retreated only to recruit his forces, as indeed he probably had done. The regent therefore resolved to break for ever the power of the island chief, and, raising a numerous army, attacked him in his strongholds with such determination that Donald was compelled, in the following year, to crave for peace. This was granted on Albany's terms. The haughty Lord of the Isles gave up all claim to the earldom of Ross, and, abandoning his pretensions of independence, agreed to become a vassal of the crown of Scotland.

He kept his word more or less strictly. But his son, Alexander, rebelled in his turn, some fifteen years after Harlaw, invading the mainland, where he burned down the royal burgh of Inverness. James I was now firmly on the throne of Scotland, determined to make "the key keep the castle and the bush the cow." The king marched north with all his force, and completely routed the rebel army.

Some months after came the pitiful final appearance of the Lords of the Isles on the stage of Scottish history. When Alexander sought to make submission to the king, James would accept it only on the most humiliating conditions.

In the chapel of Holyrood, the king, with the queen and his principal nobles, stood in front of the high altar, and there was brought before him a wretched-looking man, unshaven and unkempt, clad only in his shirt, and bearing a sword in his hands. It was Alexander of the Isles, the descendant of kings. He fell on his knees before James, and there delivered up his sword, praying humbly for mercy, seeking no more than his life.

He was pardoned; but was put for a while, for safe keeping, into Tantallon Castle, to remain there until the king felt that the pride and the power of the Isles had been shattered. Then he was allowed to creep home again.

Our greatest victory fought on French soil

BAUGÉ

(22nd March, 1421.)

DURING the long course of the wars between Scotland and England, of the victories achieved by the Scots the greatest, of course, was Bannockburn, and next to it must be ranked Stirling Bridge. The third was fought neither on Scottish soil nor on English, but over the sea in Normandy, where an army of Scots in the French service inflicted on the troops of the mighty Henry V the first reverse they sustained during their invasion of France.

Scotsmen had fought for the kings of France long before that time, and continued to do so for long after it. For centuries they formed a regular part of the French army, in which it was that the Royal Scots, the First Regiment of Foot, saw their earliest service. The Scots Guard was looked on as the élite of the troops of France, acting as the royal bodyguard almost till the time of the Revolution.

Tradition would have it that the Auld Alliance dates back to times of the most remote antiquity. It may do, but the earliest definite record of a treaty between Scotland and France is no older than the period of David II. The alliance was then brought about by the aggressive policy pursued by Edward III of England against the two countries.

When Charles le Bel died, in 1328, Edward, in defiance of the Salic law, claimed the French throne in right of his mother, who had been Charles's sister. The French people repudiated him, and chose Philip of Valois for their king, to the intense annoyance of Edward, one of whose main characteristics was greed. For a while he appeared to suffer his rebuff patiently; but, in 1337, he quartered the golden lilies of France with the English leopards on his shield, assumed the motto, "Dieu et mon Droit," pawned the crown and the royal jewels, seized all the wool and tar in his kingdom, and with the proceeds raised an army and sailed for France. At Sluys and at Crecy he gained victories that in any other cause would have been glorious, instead of, as they were, the lamentable successes of a criminal attack upon the freedom of a nation.

In his distress, Philip of France appealed for help to the king of Scots, David II, who, during the troublous period of his minority, had found shelter at the French court. An offensive and defensive alliance was entered into, of which the immediate result to Scotland was the disaster at Neville's Cross and the capture of her king, small misfortune though the latter was.

During the remainder of the Hundred Years War, and for long after it, large bodies of Scottish soldiers served in the French forces and played a distinguished part in the struggle against English aggression. At Poitiers, the Scots corps, along with the German cavalry, were given the costly honour of forming the first line. Theirs it was to meet the first shock of the charge of the English men-at-arms, and almost to a man they were cut down. Their leader, Lord William Douglas, was wounded, but escaped the fate of his brother, Sir Archibald, who was made prisoner. In his account of the fight, Froissart says, "And also in the kynges batayle there was therl Dugles of Scotland, who fought a season right valyantly, but, when he saw the disconfyture, he departed and saved hymselfe, for in no wyse he wolde be taken of the Englyeshmen; he had rather ben there slayne."

Frequent appeals to Scotland came from Philip's successors, John and Charles V, for help in their wars. These were made because they "knew well that all the realme ther had mortell hate to thenglysshmen, for these two realmes coude never love togyder." The king of England "was sore displeased, for he doubted more the warre of the Scottes than of the Frenchmen; for he knew well the Scottes loved hym not."

In June, 1377, died that dread warrior, the third Edward of England, after a career of rapine and bloodshed and a lifetime wasted in vain pursuit of empire. His country made peace with France, but not for long. Henry V revived the old pretensions, and once more an English army crossed the Channel, to inflict on the French a crushing defeat at Agincourt.

Another appeal was made to Scotland, imploring aid. A parliament was summoned, and the Estates decided that, since the safety of Scotland was so much bound up in the independence of France, a strong force should be sent to the relief of their allies. Under the earl of Buchan, an army embarked in ships provided by Castile and Aragon, and, in spite of the attempt of an English fleet to intercept them, landed safely at la Rochelle. With Buchan were the flower of the Scottish nobility, Archibald Douglas, earl of Wigtown and afterwards Marshall of France, Sir Alexander Buchanan of that ilk, Sir John Stewart of Darnley, Sir Henry Cunningham of Kilmaurs, Sir John Swinton of that ilk, Sir Hew Kennedy, and a host of others, all well experienced in war.

When the Scottish force arrived in France, the English king had left the 'country for a time, entrusting the command of his troops to his brother, the duke of Clarence, a very gallant soldier. Clarence was engaged in an attempt to clear the French out of Normandy.

He came on the Scottish army, with some French troops attached to it, near the little town of Baugé, about twenty miles from Angers. Between the two forces ran the river Couanon, at that point deep and rapid, with only a narrow bridge by which it might be crossed. For the bridge Clarence made straight, at the head of a picked body of men-at-arms. But Sir Robert Stewart of Railston, with a small band of thirty bowmen, stood in his way, and from a church close by

Sir Hew Kennedy rushed out with a hundred more.
With a flanking shower of arrows they drove the English
back.   Then dashed forward two hundred chosen knights
under Buchan himself, and a fight without quarter
began in the narrow passage of the bridge.   Inspired by
the hate of centuries, the English and Scots fought like
madmen.   "The former," says Buchanan, "took it in
great disdain that they should be attacked by such an
implacable enemy, not only at home but beyond the
seas."

Beguiled by fatal vanity, Clarence wore round his
helmet his golden coronet; and he was instantly the mark
of every lance.   Sir John Swinton wounded him in the
face; a moment later Sir John Carmichael spurred on
him so furiously that the stout ash of his lance was
shivered on the prince's corselet; then, as Clarence was
falling from his horse, Buchan, eager for a share in the
glory, dashed out his brains with an iron mace.

Enraged by the fall of their leader, the English fought
with redoubled fury, disputing every foot of the crossing,
till they were cut to pieces by the merciless Scots.   Then,
the bridge won, the victors pressed over the river, and
fell on the main body of the enemy, attacking them
fiercely with sword and lance, and putting them to rout.

Seventeen hundred Englishmen fell at Baugé.   The
losses of the Scots and French were trifling.

Honours were showered on those who had distinguished
themselves in the fight.   The earl of Buchan had bestowed
on him the sword and office of Constable of France,
and as such was second in rank and authority only to the
king himself.   He received, besides, the princely domain
of the whole territory between Chartres and Avranches.
Stewart of Darnley was granted the lordship of Aubigné.
The king of France added to the shield of Sir Hew
Kennedy, in memory of his defence of the bridge, azure,
three fleurs-de-lys or; and to Sir John Carmichael's, a
hand grasping a broken spear, for his unhorsing of
Clarence.

The battle of Baugé for a time curbed the progress of Henry's arms in France, and it led the way to the victories of La Pucelle and the ultimate expulsion of the invaders. The Scottish soldiers who won it were not mercenaries, as they are so often described as being, but were troops engaged in the service of an ally of their country. Their action and their success so enraged the king of England that he compelled his prisoner, James I of Scotland, to accompany the English army, then hanged as a rebel every Scot whom he captured in the field, an action whose only effect was to strengthen the hearts of Buchan's heroes for their task.

Great as were the achievements of the living Scots in France, a greater was wrought by a dead one, if we are to believe the historians of the fifteenth century. Henry was himself at the head of his army again, and set his men to pillage for food. Among other acts of rapine, he ordered the plunder of the shrine of Saint Fiacre, the holy son of an ancient Scottish king. For this sacrilege he was smitten by the saint with a kind of leprosy, and shortly died of it, cursing the Scots, and lamenting that "je ne puis aller nulle part sans trouver devant ma barbe des Ecossais morts ou vifs."

The number of Scots, of the best blood of their country, who died for France's freedom can never be computed. Thousands were lost at Crevant and Verneuil and Roverai, three bloody fights in which, almost unsupported by the men whose cause they were championing, they faced the power of England, three defeats that brought as great honour as victory. The main striking force of France, they conquered at Pathay and Montepilloy. They formed the most part of the garrison that held Orleans for seven months till it was relieved by Joan of Arc. At various times the earl of Buchan, the earl of Douglas, and Stewart of Darnley were entrusted with the supreme command of the French forces. All three of them gave their lives for France, as did countless thousands of their countrymen.

For Scotland the Auld Alliance is a thing to be remembered only with pride.

VERNEUIL (17th August, 1424).—While the duke of Bedford was carrying on the war in France on behalf of his young nephew, Henry VI of England, his army was encountered near the little town of Verneuil by a force of which the main body consisted of ten thousand Scots. In a bloody battle the Scots were almost exterminated. The few of them who survived were formed into the regiment which was later to become so famous in French history as the Scots Guard.

SARK (23rd October, 1448).—In the reign of James II there was almost constant Border warfare between Scotland and England, carried on mainly by the two rival houses of Douglas and Percy. In 1448, the earl of Northumberland crossed the Border with an army of 5000 men. On the bank of the river Sark, near Gretna, he met a slightly smaller force under the earl of Ormond, brother of the Douglas. The Englishmen were put to rout. Five hundred of them are said to have been drowned in the river, and an immense number, including the younger Percy, were made prisoners.

LOCHMABEN (22nd July, 1484).—Through all his reign James III was harassed by revolting subjects. The principal offenders were his brother, the duke of Albany, and the "Black Douglas." These two entered into correspondence with the king of England, Richard III, and endeavoured to persuade him to invade Scotland. Having failed in this, they raised themselves a small force of English troops and rode into Dumfriesshire, hoping that their friends would rally there to their support. At Lochmaben they were defeated by a Scottish force under some of the local gentry. Albany escaped to France. Douglas was made prisoner, and condemned to end his life as a monk in the abbey of Lindores.

SAUCHIEBURN (11th June, 1488).—The crushing of the revolt of Albany and Douglas only stemmed for a space

the tide of rebellion in Scotland. The third James was
perhaps the most unfortunate of Scottish kings. A
man of peaceful pursuits, he had an unhappy talent for
giving offence to his nobles, who, in ever increasing
numbers, lost all sympathy with him and determined to
drive him from the throne. By 1488 these insurgents
had reached such strength that they were able to take
the field with a large army. The king raised another,
and the two forces met at Sauchieburn, close to the
field of Bannockburn. They were well matched, and for
a while the issue was in doubt; but at last, despairing of
victory, the king fled and his army scattered. James
took refuge in a nearby mill, thinking to lie concealed
there till he might escape under the cover of night.
What happened next will never be truly known; but
the king's body was found in the mill, steeped in blood,
with a dagger through the heart.

Battles at Sea!

THERE is a very common tendency to imagine that Scotland has no naval history, that she never, in fact, possessed such a thing as a fleet. It is true that her achievements in naval warfare have been few, and possibly slight; but it would be a strange thing indeed if the race which produced so many of the hardy seafarers who manned the armed trawlers and drifters that protected our coasts during the Great War had never aspired to naval eminence.

Robert the Bruce appears to have been the first Scottish king to realise that a country with so extensive a seaboard as ours cannot depend for its safety entirely on a military force, but must be prepared to meet its enemies on the sea as well as on land. He established the beginnings of a Scottish navy, building several men-of-war which were able to hold their own with any others of their time.

During the reigns of the successors of Bruce, we have occasional glimpses of Scottish ships of war and of engagements on the high seas during the wars with England. It was not, however, until the time of James IV that any serious attempt was made at building such a fleet as would entitle Scotland to rank among the naval powers of Europe.

James was a man of ambition and enterprise. His imagination was fired by the discovery of America, and the voyages of the Portuguese navigators. There were apparently all manner of new worlds to be discovered and conquered, and Scotland, as well as any other, might have her share in the glory and the spoil. She had men as good as any Spaniards or Portuguese; she must now have the ships. So the king decided, and his subjects were willing to back him in the enterprise.

Already in the time of his father there had been a group of sea-captains of some small renown in Scotland. They were only traders, it is true, but so also were Hawkins and Drake when they laid the first foundations of England's glory on the seas. Merchant seamen of the fifteenth and sixteenth centuries were more than sailors. They had not only to transport their cargoes, but to protect them from the pirates and freebooters who infested every ocean. Their ships were armed, and they knew how to fight them as well as to sail them.

The captains to whom James turned for help in his ambitious scheme were Andrew Wood of Largo, and the family of the Bartons, John, the father, and his three sons, Andrew, Robert and John, all daring seamen and stout-hearted fighters. With their guidance, and the enthusiastic support of his people, the king laid down keel after keel in dockyards on the Forth, until he had a navy which included the largest ship then afloat on the sea. Sir Andrew Wood was made admiral of the fleet.

Wood had been a merchant trader of simple origin before he was given a title and estates by James III in reward for his services as "pilot" to that monarch. He possessed two ships of his own, the *Flower* and the *Yellow Caravel*, each of about three hundred tons, large vessels for those days, well manned and fitted, and armed with a weight of ordnance much beyond what was common at that time. Although employed as trading vessels, they were in effect highly efficient men-of-war. These ships were Wood's own property; but they were in the royal service. One of the conditions, indeed, of their owner's tenure of Largo was that they should be kept constantly in good repair. It was on them that the Scots fought their first recorded naval action against an English squadron.

In 1489, a fleet of five English vessels entered the Firth of Forth and inflicted considerable damage on the coast towns of Fife and the Lothians, which they raided and looted. As there was a truce between Scotland and England, this was an act of piracy, which could not be allowed to go unpunished. The king ordered Sir Andrew Wood to pursue the raiders and bring them to action, a command which the old sea-dog was only too happy to obey.

The *Flower* and the *Yellow Caravel* set sail, and, coming on the Englishmen off Dunbar, at once engaged them, in no way perturbed by their superiority in number. The English crews put up a stout fight, but in the end they were forced to strike their flags and yield themselves prisoners to the Scots, who brought their five prizes triumphantly into the port of Leith and handed them over to the king.

The king of England, Henry VII, was furious when he heard of what had happened, though he had no cause to be, for his men had been clearly at fault. He vowed that he would have vengeance on Andrew Wood, and offered a huge reward to any of his mariners who would bring him the bold Scot, dead or alive.

A merchant-adventurer of London, one Stephen Bull, offered to make the attempt. Three ships were provided to him for the purpose, and on them were embarked crews of picked seamen, with archers and spearmen, and a numerous company of volunteers, knights and squires, eager to have a share in the adventure.

Bull's squadron made for the mouth of the Firth of Forth, and lay concealed behind the Isle of May, to wait the arrival of Wood's two ships, which were known to be on their way home from Flanders. When the *Flower* and the *Caravel* came into the Firth, they found the Englishmen across their path. But Sir Andrew was not taken by surprise at the sight of enemies; no good seaman of his day would have been. His guns were primed; his men were ready; and his ships were never else than prepared for action.

With flags flying defiantly at their mastheads, the

white cross of Saint Andrew and the red cross of Saint George, the two fleets drew together. Naval tactics in the fifteenth century were of the crudest, the only thought being to bring the opposing vessels quickly to grips, and to fight it out, hand to hand, on the bulwarks and decks. As Wood's ships came up, therefore, they were run alongside the Englishmen, who had made known their hostile intent by the discharge of a cannonade. Grappling irons were quickly made fast, and the ships were locked tightly together.

The fight began soon after sunrise, and lasted all through a long summer day. With swords and pikes, muskets and bows, the combatants struggled for the mastery. On the decks men fought breast to breast. In the riggings sharpshooters picked off their enemies with bolt and ball. Fortune veered now one way now the other. And evening found the battle still undecided, though the deck of every ship was sodden with gore and littered with dead and dying. The English had the superiority in numbers, the Scots in experience of war; for valour, all were of the bravest blood in this island.

When darkness fell, the grapples were loosened, and the ships drew off, to await the morning and the renewal of the fight. Through the night they lay not far apart, and with the first gleam of daylight they rushed together again. The ships were lashed to each other with cables, and once more the battle began.

With hacking swords and thrusting pikes those determined foes strove for the victory, fighting for the honour of the red cross and the white. Backward and forward swayed the battle, now on one ship, now on another.

The vessels were left to move with the wind and the tide, while their crews were at each other's throats; presently they had drifted far from the Forth and into the mouth of the Tay. There the inhabitants of the neighbouring villages lined the shores, cheering their champions, and calling loudly on Saint Andrew to stand by his people.

Their prayer was answered. Wood's men won the day in the end, and forced the Englishmen to strike their colours. The London ships were carried into the port of Dundee; while Stephen Bull and his principal officers, or such at least of them as survived, were taken to Edinburgh and presented as prisoners to the king.

Chivalrous as always, James received them in a fashion which probably they had little looked for. He praised their valour, loaded them with gifts, and sent them home in their own vessels, with a message to the king of England that Scotland had both ships and men capable of defending her shores against any aggression. A hint was added, that future raiders might not find themselves quite so gently dealt with.

For many more years Andrew Wood played a leading part in Scotland, both as admiral and statesman. In his old age he retired to his estate at Largo, but he refused to be parted altogether from the sea and ships. He had a canal dug from his house to the parish church, and along it he was rowed every Sunday in a barge by his old boat's crew.

Second in fame only to Andrew Wood himself were the Barton brothers. They had salt water in their veins, for their father was a seaman before them.

The elder Barton was plundered—some say murdered —by the Portuguese. His family appealed to the king of Scots for redress, and, representations to the court of Portugal having proved of no avail, letters of marque were granted to the Bartons, authorising them to take satisfaction from any Portuguese vessels they might encounter in their voyages. This they proceeded to do with right good will, soon reimbursing themselves, and more, for all the loss their father had suffered.

The most noted of the three brothers was Andrew, who owned a ship named the *Lion*, one of the largest vessels of her day. His position is somewhat difficult to define. He was a merchant seaman, he carried on a

private war with Portugal, and at times he was employed
by the king in commissions of a purely naval character.
In a later age he would have been described, perhaps, as a
privateer.

He was a skilled seaman and a fierce fighter, and
whatever he did he did it thoroughly, as witness one
episode in his career as a servant of the king. Some
Dutch ships set out on one of the piratical cruises in
which almost all seafarers occasionally indulged at that
time and plundered a number of Scottish vessels,
butchering those crews who dared to resist them. King
James entrusted Barton with the task of bringing the
offenders to book, giving him a strong squadron for
the purpose. Andrew sailed away south, and came in
due time on the pirates, whom he had little difficulty in
putting out of action. Then, to save the time and
trouble of a trial, he put all the captured Dutchmen
to death, and pickled their heads in their own salt-beef
casks, to be brought to Scotland as evidence that he
had faithfully fulfilled his commission.

From that day Barton had not only Portugal but
Holland also at war with him. England was shortly to
be added to the number. How exactly it came about is
somewhat obscure, although the pope, among others, has
been blamed for it. All that is definitely known is that,
for whatever reason, the king of England was persuaded to
declare that Andrew Barton must be driven off the seas.
The two finest ships in the English navy, commanded
by Lord Thomas Howard and his brother, Sir Edward
Howard, were therefore fitted out for war and sent to
look for the daring Scot. They had not far to seek
for him. Near the Downs they came on the *Lion* and
a tiny consort, a pinnace, the *Jenny Pirwen*, returning
from a cruise against the Portuguese.

The Howards fired a broadside as a challenge, and
Barton willingly accepted it, although the force against
him was so greatly superior to his own. He brought
his ships alongside the Englishmen, and grappled them.

Then the fight began, with the utmost ardour on both sides.

One of Barton's favourite devices was an ancient Roman one. Heavy weights were suspended from the yardarms of his ships. When these were in a favourable position, overhanging an enemy vessel, the weights were cut loose, in the hope that the force they gained in their fall would carry them through the bottom of the other craft and so sink her.

When the *Lion* was closely locked with Lord Howard's ship, Barton gave the order for one of the weights to be let go. To do this, a man had to go aloft. Two of his seamen made the attempt, but each was brought down by an English archer, the best bowman among them, who had been detailed to prevent the manoeuvre. Then Barton sprang into the shrouds, determined to go up to the yardarm himself. Howard recognised him by his rich dress and the gold chain he wore.

"Now, on your life," cried the English captain to his bowman, "shoot true!"

"An' I were to die for it," said the archer, "I have but two arrows left."

They were enough. The first one bounded harmlessly off Barton's mail. But the second found a gap in his armour, at the armpit, as he stretched up his hand to grasp a ratline above his head.

He fell back on the deck; but raised himself to his feet again, unwilling that his men should know how sorely wounded he was.

"Fight on!" he cried to them. "Fight on! Stand ye fast by the Cross of Saint Andrew!"

They were his last words. He had scarce uttered them, when he fainted from loss of blood; and soon he died.

The English were exultant; the Scots dismayed. Howard led a boarding party on to the *Lion*, and carried everything before him. Soon the two Scottish ships were in his hands, to be taken in triumph to London.

Andrew Barton was not left unavenged. King James granted to his brothers letters of reprisal, and they were made good use of. Robert Barton set out with a Scottish squadron, and ere long returned to Leith with thirteen English prizes following meekly after him. Even then the king was not satisfied. In the message which he sent to Henry VIII before the commencement of the Flodden campaign, amongst the grievances which were detailed as a sufficient cause for war, one of the principal was "that Andrew Barton had been slaughtered and his ships unjustly captured by an English admiral."

Shortly before the despatch of this cartel, there had put to sea, to the assistance of France, a Scottish fleet, from the account of which we can form a fair estimate of the strength of James IV's navy. It consisted of twenty-seven vessels, of which one was the famous *Great Michael*, and thirteen others were "ships of three tops," in the naval parlance of the period. Three thousand men were carried on this formidable armada.

The *Great Michael* was the wonder of her day, the largest vessel then afloat. She was two hundred and forty feet long and fifty-six feet broad, while her stout sides are said to have been no less than ten feet thick, of solid oak. To provide the beams and planks for her, all the forests of Fife were exhausted, unless Falkland wood, besides much timber brought from Norway. She was armed with thirty-six heavy guns and three hundred smaller pieces of ordnance; while her crew consisted of three hundred sailors, one hundred and twenty gunners, and a thousand other fighting men. When she was tested by firing cannon at her at close range, the balls rebounded harmlessly from her sides. Her captain was Sir Andrew Wood, and his first lieutenant Robert Barton.

With such a fleet, and it was only in its infancy, James IV might have made himself the master of the seas had he not embarked on the ill-advised and ill-fated campaign that ended at Flodden. As it was, his death saw the end of Scottish naval ambition. Most of his ships, including the *Great Michael*, were sold by the regent Albany to France, and none of his successors was gifted with his vision of the importance of sea power.

The Great Michael, 1511

Glorious memory from a disastrous defeat

FLODDEN.

(9th September, 1513.)

KING JAMES the Fourth of Scotland never loved his
brother-in-law, the eighth Henry of England. There
were many reasons, of which possibly not the least potent
was the fact that Henry, in spite of heated protests, had
withheld a portion of his sister's dowry. There was
constant friction between the two kings, and frequent
passages at arms, both on land and sea, between their
subjects, although in name their countries were at
peace. From the date of Henry's accession, it had been
obvious to all the world that sooner or later there would
be war again between England and Scotland.

Things came to a head in 1513. In June of that year
Henry invaded France on a trifling pretext, and the
French king besought the king of Scots for support, an
appeal that met with ready sympathy. Not only did
the king of France write to James, but the queen also.
Well aware of his almost fantastically romantic nature,
she referred to him as a gallant knight, the protector
of dames, and to herself as a damsel in distress, whose
life and honour were threatened by the designs of a
treacherous foe; and implored him, for her sake, to
advance into England, were it but three steps, as a
token of defiance of Henry and promise of succour for
France. This letter was accompanied by a ring from
her own fair finger.

Difficult as it is to-day to understand how any king
should be willing to commit his country to war on the
strength of such an appeal, there is no doubt that it
exercised a powerful influence on James, who was a
survival, in the sixteenth century, of the days of romantic
chivalry. Besides, his own quarrels with Henry made

him easy to persuade to take the field against that
monarch.

He summoned all the forces of his kingdom to meet
him on the Borough Muir of Edinburgh in the third week
of August. The wisest heads in Scotland were all
against the projected war; yet the fighting men answered
the call without demur. Probably they were as anxious
as the king could be to strike another blow at the old
enemy. The barons collected their vassals, the burghs
their freemen, and a mighty host it was that assembled on
the appointed day.

Strange things happened while the army was gathering. One evening at vespers, James was worshipping
in one of the side chapels of the church of St. Michael,
which adjoined his palace of Linlithgow, when out of the
shadows, no one could say from where, there appeared
a venerable man, clad in a long blue cloak, his hair hang-
ing to his shoulders, and a look of majesty on his face.
Going up to the king, who was kneeling at a desk, the
stranger leaned over him, and, in solemn tones, warned
him to desist from the purpose he was bent on, and to
beware of the counsels of women. Then, as suddenly
as he come, the old man disappeared again amid the
crowd of people in the church, while, restrained by
superstitious fear, none of the king's attendants made
any effort to hinder him. A man they would have
tackled, but not a phantom.

The episode, which is well attested, had not the slightest
effect on the king. Perhaps he put it down as a
theatrical device of the queen's, as probably it was.

Another event, this time in Edinburgh, was even
more weird. When the army was assembled on the
Borough Muir, a voice was heard one midnight, at the
Mercat Cross, summoning by name all the lords and
gentlemen who, within forty days, would be called on
for their life's reckoning. Many people heard it, men
honest beyond question. The names of the doomed
were remembered, and, of all who were summoned,

only one there was who did not die at Flodden, one who, by a happy chance, was not present at the battle.

This second warning, however much one may suspect the genuineness of its supernatural origin, might have been expected to alarm the more credulous of James's followers into wholesale desertion. There is no record, however, of the defection of a single man of any importance.

On the 22nd August the Scottish army crossed the Tweed and began to lay siege to Norham Castle, one of the strongest fortresses in the north of England. Six days later the castle fell, carried by assault during a stormy night of wind and rain. This early success was soon followed by others. Within another week the castles of Wark, Etal and Ford were in the hands of the Scots. James was wasting no time in his effort to create a diversion which would ease the pressure on France.

Meanwhile the earl of Surrey, who had been entrusted by Henry with the care of the Border, was making his way laboriously northward with his army, over roads that were little better than quagmires, in which his waggons stuck and his horses foundered. On the 3rd of September he was at Alnwick, where next day he was joined by his son, Lord Thomas Howard, High Admiral of England, the man who had defeated Andrew Barton.

That day Surrey sent to James, by the mouth of a herald, Rouge Croix, a message challenging him to battle and requesting him "to tarry for the same." James replied, two days later, by Islay Herald, that battle was what he had come into England for, and "that he would abide him (Surrey) there till Friday (9th) at noon." Surrey agreed that Friday would be a suitable day, and promised to be promptly in the field. It was all like arranging an encounter at some sport.

The preliminaries thus adjusted, the Scots took up their position on Flodden Hill, an eminence overlooking the Till, while Surrey went into camp at Wooler Haugh, some six miles away. It was still three days from the rendezvous. These were spent by both sides in such preparations as were possible in the wild unseasonable weather that had continued from the beginning of the campaign.

Surrey sent scouts to spy out his enemies' position, and they brought back to him a piece of startling news. The Scots had established themselves in a natural fortress. They were on a hill. On their left was the river; on their right a marshy plain, full of bogs, and thick with reeds. The only possible approach was by the slope which lay in front of them, facing southwards towards the English, and across the foot of this a ditch had been dug and a parapet thrown up, with the muzzles of their guns leering across it. It was to be Halidon Hill over again, with the odds all on the other side this time.

Surrey was decidedly peeved. He felt that a scurvy trick had been played on him, for, while he was quite willing to meet the Scots in fair battle, he had no desire, worthy man, to have to charge their guns before he could get at the men, and then to attack them solely by a frontal assault up a hill, with no possibility of a flanking movement by his cavalry.

On the 7th, he sent Rouge Croix off again with another message, a request so absurdly Gilbertian in its impudence that it could have been prompted only by James's reputation for exaggerated chivalry. After complaining that the Scottish king had not kept to his bargain, in which, it was held, a fair field was implied, but "had since put himself into a ground more like a fortress or camp than upon any indifferent ground for battle to be tried," Surrey suggested that on the following day the Scots should come down to the level ground below the hill, where the English would be prepared to meet them between mid-day and three o'clock in the afternoon. James was requested to confirm that arrangement by nine o'clock the next morning so that all might be made ready.

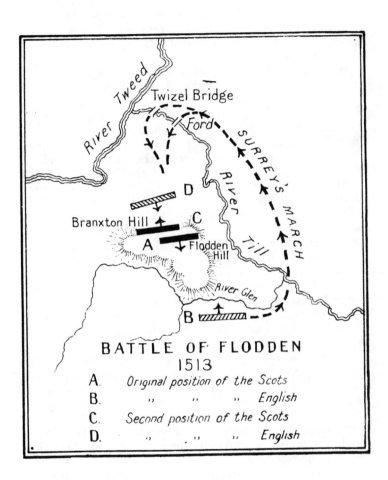

BATTLE OF FLODDEN
1513

A.   Original position of the Scots
B.   ,,   ,,   ,,   English
C.   Second position of the Scots
D.   ,,   ,,   ,,   English

James's reply was short and to the point. He would "take and keep his ground and field at his own pleasure." If only he had kept to that sensible resolution, the story of Flodden would have been a very different one from what it is; it would probably have been a second Bannockburn.

Having failed in the meantime to persuade James to come down from his height, Surrey, who apparently felt himself still bound by his agreement to attack the Scots on Friday, the 9th, called a council of his principal commanders, and among them they decided that their forces should march round the Scottish position, cross the Till at Twizel Bridge, close to the Border, and place themselves between the Scots and the Tweed.

The relative strengths of the two armies is a question that has been much debated and will never be settled. "The Trewe Encountre or Batayle lately don between Englande and Scotlande," a contemporary pamphlet, puts Surrey's army at 26,000 of all arms, a figure which may be accepted as probably correct, in spite of estimates by later writers, running to 50,000 and more. As to the Scots, Pitscottie gives their numbers as 100,000. while Buchanan holds that they were less than 20,000. The probability is that the forces may have been roughly about equal in numbers, each amounting to something over 20,000 men.

There is no record as to the English artillery, but it is known to have been much inferior to the Scottish, which numbered seventeen guns, seven of them curtals and culverins, the Seven Sisters, so heavy that each piece required thirty-six oxen to drag it along. They were among the finest specimens of artillery of their time. made all of brass, and notable not only for their size but for their beautiful workmanship.

The main part of the English were armed with their traditional bills and bows. The Scots carried mostly long pikes and, as usual, had very few bowmen. Both sides fought all the day on foot.

Scots artillery mangled by English round shot

The clash of sword and spear

Such then were the two armies that faced each other on
Friday, the 9th of September, 1513. Early that morning
the English moved northward along the Till from Bar-
moor Wood, and the vanguard and artillery began to
cross the river by Twizel Bridge, while the main body
passed over a ford about a mile further up the stream.

And all the while, James, turned from his original
purpose by a sudden romantic whim, remained inactive
on the hill of Flodden. In vain his most trusted coun-
sellors besought him to fall on the enemy while their force
was broken and confused in the crossing of the river. In
vain Borthwick, his master of artillery, fell on his knees,
and implored to be allowed to take his guns forward and
bring them into action against the men who were swarm-
ing over the bridge and the ford. Victory was in the hands
of the Scots, if they seized the opportunity they were
given; and everyone who pointed out that fact to the
king had only a gruffly rude reply for his reward.

To the earl of Angus, that sage old warrior "Bell-the-
Cat," James said, "If you are afraid, Angus, you may
go home." Lord Lindsay of the Byres was told that if
he spoke another word he would be hanged, on the
return to Scotland, in front of his own castle gate. With
James, indeed, it seemed to be truly the case that whom
the gods will destroy they first make mad. He had
decided to throw away his advantage, and to allow
Surrey to cross the river unhindered and draw up his
army at his leisure in array for battle.

Surrey's object in crossing the Till at Twizel was to
get to the rear of the Scots and occupy Branxton Hill,
a gentle-sloped eminence somewhat to the north of
Flodden Hill, which it closely adjoined. When the
most part of his army was over the river, a start was
made towards this manoeuvre. Then at last James
consented to take some action. He gave orders for a
move towards Branxton Hill, in the hope of reaching it
ahead of the English. Before leaving their position on
Flodden, his men set fire to the huts of branches and

rushes in which they had been living there; then cheerfully they set off, in high confidence of a happy outcome to their adventure.

From the burning huts arose a thick cloud of dense smoke, which rolled down the northern slope of the hill and formed a screen between the two armies. When it had cleared away they were revealed to each other in the neighbourhood of Branxton, with only about a quarter of a mile between them. The Scots were on Branxton Hill, the English at the foot of the very gentle slope in which it falls away to the north and east.

James drew up his army in five divisions. He himself commanded the centre; on the left were the divisions of Home and Huntly; on the right those of Lennox and Argyll. Behind the centre was a reserve, commanded by Bothwell, which later came up between the king and Lennox. The English formation was in two lines to begin with. In the van, Lord Thomas Howard commanded the centre, with his brother Edmund on his right and Sir Marmaduke Constable on his left. In the rear, the centre was commanded by Surrey himself, the right by Lord Dacre, and the left by Sir Edward Stanley. After the first shock of the battle, these all came up into line with the vanguard.

The English were facing south, the Scots towards their own country. The weather was unsettled, with alternate spells of sunshine and rain; and the ground was so sodden and slippery that many of the men, on both sides, cast off their shoes and fought in their socks, for better foothold.

Between four and five in the afternoon the battle began. First there was a short artillery duel, in which, despite the greater size and number of the Scottish guns, the English had the advantage, many men in James's division being mangled and slain by the round-shot of stone and iron. Posted as they were on a hillside, the Scottish pieces could not be depressed sufficiently to enable them to make effective play on their enemies.

It was not for long that the cannonading lasted. James was eager to come to close quarters with his foes, and ordered an advance of his whole line down the hillside. The first collision took place on the Scottish left, which was much closer than the rest of the line to the English, the Scots being formed up, more or less, in echelon of divisions from left to right.

The men under Huntly and Home made a furious rush on the English right, attacking Edmund Howard's division, which was soon thrown into confusion and completely routed. Only with the greatest difficulty did Sir Edmund himself manage to escape with his life leaving his banner trampled in the mire.

To save the situation, Dacre brought forward his division, which was immediately behind Edmund Howard's. He was met by the next part of the Scottish line, under the earls of Crawford and Montrose. The Scots had advanced steadily with levelled spears, and a desperate conflict ensued, the English bills striving to hew their way through the ranks of the Scots, who held resolutely to their ground.

In the centre, James, with consummate gallantry but complete disregard of the duties of a commander, had put himself in the front rank, a bodyguard of his nobles on each side of him. He led his division straight for the English centre, making himself for the standard of Surrey, who had now come up abreast of his son. The first shock of the attack carried the Scots right through the foremost ranks of the English. James, at one moment, was almost within grasping distance of Surrey's banner; it looked for a space as if the day were already his.

Then relief came to Surrey from Dacre, who had succeeded at last in disposing of Crawford and Montrose, and now threw his division on to the flank of the Scottish centre, which wavered under this attack until Bothwell's reserve came forward and restored the balance.

On the Scottish right, the Highland clans, under

Lennox and Argyll, were sorely galled as they advanced
by the shafts of the English bowmen, against which
tartan plaids were but poor protection. Before they
came into contact with their enemies their ranks were
already broken, as they rushed wildly forward, each man
thinking only to evade the shower of arrows and to come
to sword play as speedily as possible. A disorganised
mass, they threw themselves on Constable's brigade,
where for a while they wrought havoc with their claymores. But Stanley came up and took them on the
flank. Then they broke like a wave, and melted away
in scattered groups, some still fighting desperately,
some fleeing for their lives.

This was now the situation. Home's Borderers, on the
left, had achieved a rapid success, and, failing to follow
it up, were standing inactive on the outskirts of the
battle. On the right, the Highlanders had been broken
and dispersed. In the centre, the king's division, reinforced by parties which had rallied to it from the flanks,
was maintaining itself against Surrey and Howard
and Dacre. The day was not yet lost, even though
Stanley, restraining his men from the pursuit of the
fleeing remnants of the clans, had come round to the
rear of the Scottish centre, which was now completely
ringed round by English steel.

Still James was in the forefront of the battle, fighting
with a spear until it was broken in his hands, then
drawing his sword, and struggling ever to press nearer
to the banner which marked Surrey's station in the
fight. When at last he fell, wounded by several arrows,
his left hand almost cut from his arm, his neck torn open
by a bill, he was not more than a spear's length from his
foe.

The king was dead; but the men who had stood by
his side while he lived did not desert him now. Drawing
ever closer as their ranks grew thinner, taking their
toll of English blood for every yard of ground they
yielded, they kept their line unbroken.

The stubborn spear-men still made good
Their dark impenetrable wood,
Each stepping where his comrade stood
The instant that he fell.

No thought was there of dastard flight;
Link'd in the serried phalanx tight,
Groom fought like noble, squire like knight,
As fearlessly and well.

When night came, the Scottish centre was still resolutely holding the blood-sodden ground around the banner of the dead king, by whose side, and heaped upon his body, lay the flower of his nobility. All the manhood of Scotland was there, dead with the king, or standing, ready to die, in the wall of spears.

Surrey had gained the day, but he could not feel sure of it; so, like a prudent commander, he withdrew his troops to a little distance for the night, content to leave the final issue till the morrow.

But the battle was over. In the morning only the dead remained on the field. The Scottish guns stood abandoned on the slope of Branxton Hill. On another little hill a body of about a thousand Scots had rallied. They stayed there awhile; then, realising that they were hopelessly outnumbered, they moved slowly away towards the Tweed. Surrey made no attempt to pursue them. He had gained a victory; but he had been fought to a standstill.

It was estimated that ten thousand Scots were slain that day on Branxton Hill. Besides the king, among the dead there were thirteen earls, Crawford, Montrose, Huntly, Lennox, Argyll, Errol, Atholl, Morton, Cassillis, Bothwell, Rothes, Caithness, and Glencairn, fifteen lords, the archbishop of St. Andrews, the king's son, the bishops of Caithness and the Isles, the abbots of Inchaffray and Kilwinning, the chiefs of the Campbells and the MacLeans, the French ambassador, La Motte, and knights and squires beyond numbering. As to lesser men, there was scarce a home in Scotland that

did not have to grieve for someone lost or maimed on
Flodden Field.

Flodden was a disaster to Scotland, but it was far
from being a disgrace. Her army was not broken nor
driven to flight. It kept the field to the end, in spite of
the terrible losses it had sustained; and, when it retired,
it left behind an enemy too exhausted for pursuit.

Flodden was a disaster; it was a defeat; but it is a
glorious memory.

SOLWAY MOSS (24th November, 1542).—In the summer
of 1542, Henry VIII of England sent an army, under
the duke of Norfolk, to invade Scotland. Roxburgh
and Kelso and about twenty villages were burnt. The
king of Scots, James V, immediately decided on reprisals.
With 10,000 men he marched in November towards the
western Border. Remaining himself at Lochmaben,
he sent his troops forward with instructions to cross the
Esk and harry the country as far as they could penetrate.
Unbelievable as it may seem, no regular commander
was appointed to act in place of the king. Between
the Water of Leven and the Esk an English force was
encountered, one considerably weaker than the Scots,
who must have had an easy victory if they had seized
their advantage. Instead, they fell into a dispute as to
leadership, and allowed their enemies to attack them
before they were formed for battle. The result was
inevitable. The Scots were soon in confusion, and were
fleeing before an army with less than half of their numbers.

"BATTLE OF THE BUTTS" (24th May, 1544).—When
the earl of Arran was appointed regent of Scotland, on
the death of James V, his great rival in the country was
the earl of Lennox. Arran favoured a French alliance,
Lennox an English one. The quarrel between them
was fought out on the Gallowmuir of Glasgow, where
the "butts," or archery targets, stood. Arran was
victorious, and Lennox had to flee to England.

Towns destroyed as the 'Rough Wooing' begins

ANCRUM MOOR.

(27th February, 1545.)

THE death of James the Fifth, of a broken heart it is said, after the disaster of Solway Moss, left Scotland torn by dissensions among the men who should have been the leaders and protectors of her people. There were disputes as to the regency, quarrels about religion, and bitter differences on the question of the French alliance.

Cardinal Beaton produced what he claimed to be the will of the late king, in which he himself and the earls of Argyll, Moray and Huntly were named as a Council of Regency during the minority of the infant Queen Mary. This document, however, was declared by the Estates to be a forgery of the cardinal's, and, according to ancient Scottish custom, the next heir to the throne after Mary, the earl of Arran, was appointed regent. That immediately divided the nobles of the kingdom into two rival factions.

The Reformation was giving trouble also. There were Catholic lords, devoted to the interests of France and Rome, and others who leant towards the new religion and favoured an alliance with its great champion, Henry the Eighth of England. Henry had deep laid schemes. He contemplated a marriage between the young queen of Scots and his infant son Edward, which would ultimately bring the whole island of Britain under a Tudor dynasty. To further that end he used every endeavour to win the support of every Scottish noble on whom he could bring his influence to bear. His chief reliance he placed on the earl of Angus, the head of the Douglases. Angus was Henry's brother-in-law;

111

he had married the widowed Margaret Tudor after the death of James IV at Flodden. The Scottish nobles who had been made prisoners at Solway Moss were also counted on for much. They were set at liberty, after having been pledged to do all in their power to further Henry's ends.

At first the plans of the English king went well. In July, 1543, a marriage treaty was signed, and peace between England and Scotland seemed to be assured. That happy prospect, however, was soon shattered. The wily Beaton was still to be reckoned with. Arran was a man of no moral strength, and the cardinal proceeded to lead him into a course of vacillation and double dealing which so exasperated the king of England that that short-tempered monarch decided to employ the argument of force when diplomacy seemed likely to fail. The "Rough Wooing" of Mary Stewart began.

On Sunday, the 4th of May, 1544, an English fleet appeared in the Forth, and an army, commanded by the earl of Hertford, landed at Newhaven. There was at hand no Scottish force fit to cope with these invaders. Leith and Edinburgh were taken without resistance. Edinburgh castle held out, but was powerless to prevent the town and the palace of Holyroodhouse being set in flames. The country for five miles around the city was laid waste; then Hertford led his men at leisure back to England, burning as they went. Musselburgh, Preston, Seton, Haddington and Dunbar were left in blackened and smouldering ruins. At the end of a fortnight, the English leader was able to report with satisfaction to his master that "the like devastation has not been seen in Scotland these many years."

So easily achieved had been the destructive success of Hertford's raid that, if not perhaps to Henry, at least to many of his nobles it seemed that Scotland at last was at their mercy. There were constant incursions by English troops into the southern counties, and, within a few months, a large area of the Border lands was completely in their possession. The abbey of Coldingham was occupied by them, and made into a fortress; and considerable numbers of Scottish Borderers were even forced into the service of the English king, being given red crosses to wear on their armour in token of their changed allegiance.

The earl of Angus was appointed by the regent to the office of lieutenant of the Borders. He had not the force, or it may have been the will, to repel the invaders; and though he made an attempt to recover Coldingham it failed.

The English Warden of the Middle March was an ambitious knight, Sir Ralph Eure, or Evers. He represented to Henry that, ill-organised though the invasion of Scotland had been, it had met with such easy success that it was obvious that a determined effort would have no difficulty in reducing the whole country south of the Forth and Clyde. Henry was quite willing that the attempt should be made, so he made Eure a grant of all the territory he could conquer in the Merse, Teviotdale and Lauderdale. This touched Angus closely. "If they come to take sasine in my lands," he vowed, "I will write the deeds on their backs with sharp pens and bloody ink." He was to be as good as his word.

Under Eure and another adventurer, Sir Brian Layton, an English force, five thousand strong, marched into Scotland, where they were joined by six hundred of the red-crossed Scottish Borderers. They came to Melrose and burned down both the town and the abbey. In the latter was the burial place of the Douglases; the tombs were desecrated and the dead insulted.

The angry indignation of Angus knew no bounds. With a small band of his vassals he made a reckless attack on the intruders; but he was easily driven off, and could do no more than keep his little force hovering on the flank of Eure's army, which continued its marauding career. Later, Angus was joined by Arran with

some more men, but still the Englishmen outnumbered
them by more than five to one.

Near the village of Ancrum, on the Teviot, there is a
moor. There Eure formed a camp, confident that the
Scots would not dare to approach him. He would pro-
ably have been right had not a piece of unlooked-for
good fortune come their way, the arrival of Norman
Leslie, master of Rothes, with twelve hundred lances,
Leslies and Lindsays. Almost on his heels, too, had
come spurring old Walter Scott of Buccleuch, with word
that he had raised his men and they were barely an
hour's march away.

With these reinforcements to the Scots, the English
superiority was reduced to little more than two to one,
odds which Angus felt could be faced with an easy mind.
The Scottish troops had been posted on a hill overlooking
Ancrum Moor. On the advice of Buccleuch, they were
withdrawn to a plain behind it, Peniel Haugh, where
they were completely hidden from the English. There
the men were dismounted, and the horses were sent
away in charge of boys and grooms, who were instructed
to make sure that their movement would be seen and
would give the impression of a retiring army.

The ruse was entirely successful. Eure saw his
opponents running away, and decided immediately to
pursue them. He sent off Sir Brian Layton with an
advance guard, and himself followed hard behind
them with his main body. In the centre he had a
thousand mounted and mail-clad men-at-arms. On one
flank were the archers, and on the other the hagbutters,
more than a thousand of each of them.

The heavy horses galloped at full speed up the hill
where the Scots had been, and the footmen, eager not
to be beaten, raced beside them. Every horse and man
was blown when the top was passed, and there, to their
amazement, they discovered not the emptying plain they
had looked for, but close in front of them a long line of
determined men with lances poised to receive them.

Bitterly must Brian Layton have rued the eagerness
with which he had led his vanguard over the hill, but
there was only one thing now that as a brave man he
could do. At the head of his horsemen he rushed on the
Scottish line. Eure, who had almost made up on him,
followed close behind. He, too, realised that any attempt
at retiral now must mean disaster. His one hope lay in
the valour of his men.

Layton's horses crashed into the waiting enemy. But
the Scots were on foot, firmly set to meet the assault, and
their spears were an ell longer than the English ones.
Half the southern saddles were emptied on the first
impact, while scarce a Scottish breast-plate was touched
by an English lance. Those who survived of Layton's
vanguard were sent reeling back on their main body,
whose ranks they broke and threw into wild confusion,
terrified horses and dismayed men all mixed in a frenzied
tangle.

Then the Scots came on, steadily, pitilessly, thirsting
for revenge for what their country had suffered.

In vain the English leaders strove to rally their men,
whose only thought was now of flight. Both Eure and
Layton were slain, and their followers fled in panic
before the remorseless spears that pressed close behind
them, striking them down as they ran, while, to add to
the horror of their plight, the six hundred Scots who had
been pressed into King Henry's service tore off their
red crosses and joined with their countrymen in attacking
the now helpless Englishmen.

Of the defeated army, eight hundred men were killed
and a thousand made prisoners, a total almost as large
as the whole force of the victors. The wonder is that
so great a number were allowed to surrender themselves
alive, for the injuries of the Scots had been so many and
so deep that they can have been in no mood for mercy.

The pursuit of the survivors of Eure's vaunted army
continued for many miles from the battlefield, the
peasantry, even the women it is said, joining like packs

of hounds in the hunting of the terror-stricken wretches,
who had thrown away both arms and armour and
scattered over the countryside in frantic search of
safety.

When Henry heard of the disaster which had befallen
the force he had sent so confidently into Scotland, he
was filled with indignation against the Scottish nobles
whom he had counted as his friends, against Angus in
particular. The Douglas was little concerned. "What!"
he exclaimed, when he heard of it. "Is my brother-in-
law offended because I have avenged the outraged tombs
of my fathers? They were better men than he; and I
could do no less, though he should seek my life for it.
But little knows King Henry the skirts of Cairntable.
I can keep myself there against all his English host."

Black Saturday —
English pursue and
slay Scots
PINKIE.

(10th September, 1547.)

In three battles Scottish armies suffered disasters, when they should instead have achieved decisive victories. In each a strong position was abandoned with insane hardihood, and the almost certainty of success thrown recklessly away. The first was Flodden and the third Dunbar; less well known than these is Pinkie, where the same mad policy was pursued.

After Ancrum, King Henry sent the savage earl of Hertford across the Tweed again, to punish the Scots for their presumption in daring to fight for their liberties. He came in September, when the harvest had just been gathered, so that he might find full scope for his destructive genius. There can have been few corn-stacks, within many miles of the Border, that escaped the flames of his torches. Five abbeys he destroyed in his fury, five market towns, sixteen castles, two hundred and forty-three villages, and an untold number of churches. The ruins of ecclesiastical buildings that bestrew the Scottish Borders are still witnesses to the wild barbarism of Hertford's raid.

Content with the devastation he had wrought, the raider went home again. No attempt was made at the actual conquest of Scotland, Henry's idea apparently being that by such demonstrations of his power he would terrify the Scots into accepting his proposals. In this he was sadly disappointed; the only effect of his policy was to drive Scotland into closer association with France.

Henry died in January, 1547. The new king, Edward VI, was a minor; and Hertford, now duke of Somerset, became Lord Protector of England. He decided to continue the methods of persuading Scotland introduced

117

by his late master, and to pursue it with even greater ferocity than ever.

Crossing the Tweed on the 2nd of September, 1547, with an army of 18,000 men, Somerset marched by the coast road towards Edinburgh. Keeping pace with him was an English fleet under Lord Clinton.

Twice on his route Somerset might have been stopped with little difficulty by even a small force of resolute men; at the deep ravine at Cockburnspath, and at the narrow bridge over the Tyne at East Linton. It took him a whole day to get his guns and his waggons over the first of those obstacles, yet no attempt was made to interfere with him. At Linton a small body of light horse appeared but were easily scattered.

The Scottish regent had exerted himself to raise an army for the defence of Edinburgh, and had succeeded in bringing together a force which is said to have been larger than Somerset's. It was assembled at Musselburgh, when, on the 8th September, the English reached the village of Preston, three miles along the coast.

Somewhat inland from Preston is an eminence known as Fawside hill. Somerset took possession of it on the morning of the 9th, and that day there was a skirmishing fight between his cavalry and a body of light Border horse, under the earl of Home. It lasted for three hours, and ended with the Scots being driven off, leaving behind them many dead and a considerable number of prisoners, including the son of their leader, who himself was severely wounded.

The position, when day broke on Saturday the 10th, was that the English were posted on Fawside hill, while the Scots faced them on an elevated plain known as Pinkie Cleuch. Between the two armies ran the Esk.

Arran had made a good selection of his ground. An account of it has been left to us by an English observer. "The plot where they lay was chosen for strength, as in all their country some thought there was not a better. It was protected on the south by a great marsh, and on

the north by the firth, which side also they fenced with
two field-pieces and certain hackbuts, lying under a turf
wall. Between us and them they were strongly defended
by the course of a river called Esk, running north into the
firth. Though it was not very deep of water, the banks
of it were so high and steep that a small sort of resistance
might have been able to keep down a great number of
comers up. About a twelve score off from the firth,
over the same river, is a stone bridge, which they did
keep also well warded with ordnance."

Somerset, who was a skilled soldier as well as a desper-
ado, must have viewed the position with some alarm. He
was facing a more difficult problem now than had ever
before confronted him during his bullying of Scotland.
The Scots were in considerable force, and occupied
ground which natural advantage and their own devices
had combined to render more like a stronghold than an
ordinary battlefield of those days. To dislodge them
must be at best both a difficult and a costly operation;
and there was a great chance that it might be altogether
impossible.

Having thus sized up the situation, the English
commander decided to venture the risk of battle. There
was grave danger in it; but so there would have been also
now in any attempt at retiral. The bold course, in spite
of its difficulties, seemed to him the better one.

As a preliminary to any attack that might be made on
Pinkie Cleuch, it was agreed by Somerset and his lieutenants that a move must first be made from Fawside to
another ridge, somewhat nearer to the enemy, from which
the Scottish position would be within cannon range.
This manoeuvre was just beginning, when an amazing
sight presented itself to the eyes of the Englishmen.
Their enemies were coming to meet them, abandoning all
their skilfully gained advantages. It seemed almost
too good to be true. Yet there was no doubt of it.
The Scottish footmen were filing over the bridge that
crossed the Esk, and drawing up in order of battle on

the near side of the river. Their cavalry, relatively small in number, had been so badly damaged in the affair of the day before that what few were left of them remained inactive on the west bank of the river. Arran was putting all his faith in his infantry.

What prompted the Scottish leader to this surprising move can only be guessed at. It is said that he decided on it in face of the protests of all his most experienced advisers, who urged that he need only remain on Pinkie Cleuch, and let the English attack him there, and victory was assured. The most likely explanation is that when Arran saw his enemies moving, he feared that they were contemplating not an attack but a retiral, and he was determined that they should not escape him.

For whatever reason it may have been, the Scottish troops had crossed the Esk, to the great relief, no doubt, of Somerset, who saw himself now on more even terms with them. He had to make haste, though, to have his columns ready for the coming battle, for so quickly had the Scots executed their manoeuvre that their crossing of the river is said to have been more like a movement of cavalry than of footmen. Soon they were drawn up in line, with their long pikes bristling in front of them.

The eye-witness already quoted gives a vivid picture of the Scottish spearmen as he saw them that day in action.

"They come to the field well furnished with jack and skull, dagger, buckler and swords, all notably broad and thin, of exceeding good temper, and all so made to slice, that, as I never saw none so good, so I think it hard to devise the better. Every man has his pike, and a great kercher wrapped twice or thrice about his neck, not for cold but for (protection against) cutting. In their array towards the joining with the enemy, they cling in the fore rank so near together, shoulder to shoulder, with their pikes in both hands straight before them, and their followers in that order so hard at their backs, laying their pikes over their foregoers' shoulders, that, if they do assail undissevered, no force can well withstand them. Standing at defence, they thrust shoulders likewise so nigh together, the fore ranks well nigh to kneeling, stooping low for their fellows behind, holding their pikes in both hands, in their left also their bucklers, the one end of the pike against their right foot, the other towards the enemy, breast high, their followers crossing their pike-points with those in front, and thus each with other so nigh as place and space will suffer, the whole mass so thick that as easily shall a bare finger pierce through the skin of an angry hedgehog as any encounter the front of their pikes."

The Scottish van was commanded by the earl of Angus. He had protested vehemently to Arran against the folly of leaving the strong position on Pinkie Cleuch, and only when ordered to do so on pain of treason had he consented to lead his men across the Esk. The "main battle" was under the direction of Arran himself. The earl of Huntly commanded the reserve. All were on foot. On the right were some pieces of artillery. On the other flank, where the cavalry might have been, was a singular assembly of warriors, a large body of monks and priests come to testify to their faith in the fight with the English heretics. Over their heads fluttered a white banner, on which was painted a symbol of the suffering Church, a woman, with dishevelled hair, who knelt in prayer before a crucifix. The motto was, "Afflictae Ecclesiae ne obliviscaris."

The earl of Warwick led the English van, Somerset the main body, and Lord Dacre the rearguard. Lord Gray was in command of the cavalry, men-at-arms and mounted Spanish carabineers. His orders were to wait until the two vanguards were engaged, and then to charge the Scots on their flank.

The first movement of the Scottish troops, once they were formed on the east side of the river, was towards the shore, with the intention, apparently, of setting themselves between Somerset's men and his ships, to which Arran seems to have believed that the English were attempting to retreat. This brought the Scots immediately under fire from the galleys. Many of them were killed or wounded, and a change of plan became obviously necessary.

Swinging his line to the right, Angus made as if he were meaning to occupy the western side of Fawside hill and so obtain the advantage of holding higher ground than his enemy. Perceiving this, Somerset altered his plans in his turn, and sent orders to Lord Gray to charge the Scottish van immediately with his men-at-arms. Thus the battle began.

As the English horsemen came thundering towards them, Angus's spearsmen halted and lowered their pikes, ready to meet the shock of the assault. So long as they stood steady in their line they were safe though they were attacked by any cavalry that could be brought against them, for Scottish pikes were eighteen feet long, and no lance or sword could ever come near the men behind them.

By an unlucky chance for Gray, Angus had drawn up his men at a spot where a boggy ditch lay between them and their enemies. Into it the English horses floundered, sinking to their hocks, and but for the gallant determination of its leader the attack might have petered out there and then. Gray was a man who was ill to daunt, however. He got his men through the bog, and rallied them on the firmer ground. Then, digging their spurs deep into their horses' flanks, they swept like a rushing wave of shimmering steel towards the bristling hedge of spears that faced them. They threw themselves on it, and in an instant ten score of English saddles were emptied.

With their pikes the Scots ripped the bellies of the horses; with their daggers they despatched the men who lay helpless on the ground.

Desperately Lord Gray strove to form up his lances for another assault, but their resolution was shaken, and

he himself was sore wounded, while bleeding and riderless
horses, plunging furiously in panic, broke the ranks of
those who had still the courage and the strength to face
the Scottish spears. The lines wavered, then wheeled
about, and galloped off to safety, breaking through the
columns of their own infantry in their flight.

Now was the time when the Scottish cavalry should
have struck, and the main body come into action. But
there was no cavalry; and Arran's and Huntly's columns
were far in the rear. Unsupported as he was, Angus
was powerless to follow up the advantage he had gained.
He had to stand still, and allow his enemies to recover
from the confusion into which he had thrown them.

Warwick was quick to avail himself of the respite he
was given. While he restored the ranks of his men-at-
arms and infantry, he sent forward his Spanish carabineers, who galloped to the edge of the ditch, and
from there, within easy range for their weapons, discharged a volley against the Scottish line. Footmen
with arquebuses joined them in the fusillade, while the
English archers sent showers of arrows whistling about
the ears of the Scots, and the English guns, posted on
a hill, dropped round shot into the thick of them.

Unable to advance, Angus was compelled to give the
order for retiral towards his supports. The movement
was begun steadily and in good order: and would doubtless have been accomplished in safety but for one unfortunate circumstance. There was a body of Highlanders
in the Scottish vanguard, Islesmen and men of Argyll.
They had played their part well enough till now: but,
when they saw the English dead and wounded lying in
front of them, they were unable to resist their instinct
for plunder. Breaking their ranks, they had run
forward to strip the bodies, and while thus engaged,
they discovered that their Lowland comrades were
moving away from them. Mistaking the nature of
the retiral, they were seized with sudden panic and fled
for their lives.

Some of the troops in the centre of the Scottish line, burghers not too well used to war, saw the fleeing Highlanders and caught the infection of terror. They dropped their spears and ran. Quickly the mad impulse spread along the line of the vanguard, and then extended to the troops in the main body and the reserve.

Where there had been a well equipped and apparently resolute force, there was now a scattering mob of panic-stricken men, throwing away their weapons and running off in every direction. All that the English had to do was to pursue and to slay.

The chase is said to have lasted from one o'clock in the afternoon till six in the evening. During those five hours of slaughter ten thousand Scots were made to pay with their lives for the folly of their commander and their own yielding to needless fears.

For long years afterwards, the day of Pinkie was remembered in Scotland as "Black Saturday." Its story is the darkest blot on the page of Scottish history, the only time when a Scottish army fled in terror before an enemy which had scarcely struck a blow.

So complete was Somerset's triumph that, if he had followed it up with energy, he must have made himself shortly the master of the greater part of Scotland. Instead, he contented himself with burning Leith and several smaller towns and villages, and seizing various castles; then, a week after the battle, he commenced his retreat to England, called there by a plot which was forming against him in the south. He was satisfied, it would appear, that the garrisons he had left behind him in the south of Scotland would have little difficulty in subduing the whole country.

Somerset had not counted on the astonishing resiliency so often shewn by the Scottish people. A new army was raised, the aid of France was enlisted, and, though the struggle was a bitter and bloody one, two years after the disaster of Pinkie the last English soldier was driven out of Scotland.

How Mary Stewart's last hopes were shattered

LANGSIDE.

(13th May, 1568.)

OF all the many battles in which Scots have fought against Scots, perhaps the only one which can be claimed to have exercised a decisive influence on the fortunes of the nation was Langside. There was much more at stake there than in any other engagement during Scotland's tragically frequent civil wars.

In considering the history of Mary Stewart, it is necessary, though perhaps not easy, to discard the veneer of romance which has accumulated around her memory. She was a woman, she was beautiful, and she may have been unfortunate, three conditions which will always win sympathy. But pity should not over-ride judgement, and, in an effort to make all allowance for Mary Stewart, do something less than justice to her enemies.

Mary's education and early life had been as unsuitable as they possibly could be for one who was to occupy the Scottish throne. In France, at the court whose ruling genius was Catherine de Medici, she had been reared in an atmosphere of Catholicism and the divine right of kings. Any democratic sympathies which she may have inherited from her father, the King of the Commons, were stifled amid the despotism of her French palaces. On the death of her husband, she came home to a Scotland where tyrants had never been tolerated, and whose religious convictions were every day becoming more determinedly opposed to the doctrines of the Church of Rome.

From the beginning, it was almost impossible that Mary's reign could ever be a happy one. She and her people were not compatible. Very early she abandoned

125

the idea of coercing them, and adopted more feminine methods of attempting to procure her ends. In this she might have been successful but for one circumstance, her devotion to the Catholic Church. Scotland would probably have been willing to accept many things, but never the restoration of the power of the priests, the one thing above all others that Mary aimed at.

The result was inevitable. On 17th June, 1567, the queen was imprisoned in Lochleven Castle, where she signed a deed of abdication. Six weeks later her son was crowned at Stirling, her half-brother, the earl of Moray, being appointed regent.

James Stewart, earl of Moray, was the son, "on the wrong side of the blanket," of James V and Margaret Erskine. He was a man of exceptional gifts, in keeping with both sides of his descent, and, if it had been his fate to be his father's heir, would have been both an able and a popular king. As it was, though an assassin's bullet cut short his career little more than two years after he had been entrusted with the government of Scotland, he is still remembered by the title of "the Good Regent."

Moray's great enemy was the duke of Chatelherault, to give the French title of which he was so proud to the head of the house of Hamilton, the earl of Arran. He was a man who makes but a poor appearance on the page of history. Before the birth of Mary's son he had been heir to the Scottish throne, and all his actions were prompted by the one thought of furthering his own interests and regal ambitions. He had been Catholic, Protestant, Catholic, and was Protestant again. While Mary was queen he had worked and plotted against her, in the hope of building his own fortunes on the ruins of hers; but his plans had been sadly disturbed by her abdication and the accession of her son, for, though he had been Mary's heir, he was not James's. His interest demanded that the queen should be set at liberty again and restored to the throne.

The first was accomplished without great difficulty. On the night of the 2nd May, 1568, Mary escaped from Lochleven. An escort, under young Lord Claud Hamilton, was waiting her, and, as fast as their horses could gallop, they carried the queen to their stronghold of Cadzow Castle. Her sympathisers had been warned to be prepared for this event. Quickly they rallied round her, so that, within a few days, she found herself with a considerable army ready to fight for her cause. Nine earls, nine bishops, eighteen lords and nearly a hundred lesser barons signed a bond pledging themselves to set her again on the throne.

Moray was in Glasgow when the news reached him of the queen's escape. With all speed he assembled as many troops as he could bring together, a force very much smaller than Mary's, but one infinitely better disciplined than the loosely knit array which had gathered at Cadzow. The townsmen of Glasgow rallied in considerable numbers to the regent's banner. They had the old score of the Battle of the Butts to wipe out against the Hamiltons.

Moray's army, which was encamped on the Burgh Muir of Glasgow, the ground which has now become Bridgeton, is said to have numbered four thousand men. Mary's was perhaps half as large again.

On the 13th of May, the regent's scouts brought word that the queen's force was moving from Hamilton in a westerly direction along the south bank of the Clyde. Her object was to reach the safety of the strong fortress of Dunbarton, which was held for her by Lord Fleming. She marched her army to Rutherglen, and then proposed to make a wide detour, to avoid Glasgow, which she knew to be strongly held by the regent's men, passing by way of Langside, Crookston and Paisley towards the river again, which she would cross by the ford a little above Dunbarton.

When Moray heard of his sister's movements, he immediately guessed at her purpose, or his spies may have

revealed it to him.   There was no time to be lost, for on
no account must the queen be allowed to reach the shelter
of Dunbarton Castle, then an almost impregnable
stronghold.   She must be brought to battle at some
favourable spot on her route.

The place chosen by Moray for the encounter was
Langside, then a little village several miles south of
Glasgow, though now a populous area well within the
bounds of the city.   Its houses and gardens stood on a
small eminence across which ran the road that Mary
must follow.

The regent's horse, under Kirkcaldy of Grange, were
despatched at the gallop to take up their position across
the road.   Behind each horseman was perched a hag-
butter.   Close behind them followed the vanguard of
the infantry, commanded by the earl of Morton, and the
regent himself with the main body.

When Grange reached Langside, he quickly made his
dispositions.   The road mounting up the hillside to the
village was a sunken one, with thick hedges on each side
of it.   Behind those hedges he posted his hagbutters.
There they were concealed from view, and could discharge
their pieces at close range on any enemy who attempted
to pass.

When Moray arrived, he was still in good time to
draw up his forces before the queen's army had appeared.
His right wing was in the village and on each side of it.
Then came the cavalry.   The left extended to the farm
of Path-head, near the highest part of what is now the
Queen's Park.   In front of the centre of the line were the
guns.

From Rutherglen, Mary marched by Blackhouse and
the Hangingshaw to Clincart Hill, now Mount Florida.
There she discovered that her way was to be disputed.

Clincart Hill is roughly equal in height to the hill of
Langside, and only a few hundred yards from it.   Between
the two there is a narrow valley.

The queen's general was the earl of Argyll, the husband

of her half-sister. He was a man of no particular ability either as a soldier or a statesman, despised by his foes and distrusted by his friends. His only idea of strategy was to rely on his superior numbers, and try to force his way straight through the ranks of his enemies.

Mary would fain have remained close by her troops while they battled for her cause, but she was persuaded to betake herself out of the way of danger. With a small escort she rode to Cathcart Castle, and, standing on a mound there, watched the wreck of her fortunes.

The engagement began with the conventional cannonade, the comparatively bloodless preamble with the guns which opened all the battles of the time. Though the distance between the two armies was so small, it is questionable whether the artillery of either side could reach the other, and certain that the fate of the day in no way depended on the exertions of the gunners. The majority of their balls of iron and stone probably fell harmlessly into the valley. The guns made a considerable din, however, and may have had their use in terrifying the novices in war.

The real battle began with the advance of the queen's vanguard. Commanded by Lord Claud Hamilton, it moved down the slope of Clincart Hill, and attempted to force the passage of the lane, now Battlefield Road, leading to Langside, the sunken way by the side of which Moray's hagbutters lay concealed. When the narrow path was well crowded with Hamiltons, the men behind the hedges opened fire, blazing right into the midst of their enemies, who were thrown into confusion, and fell back, pell-mell, into the valley again. There they were rallied, and again and again they essayed the desperate passage.

Moray's left wing was charged by the queen's cavalry, but stood its ground, and, as resolute pikemen always did, easily drove back the horsemen.

But the main fight was close to the village, in the sunken road and among the cottage gardens. There, in some places, the combatants were wedged so tightly together, pikes pushing against corselets, that one eye-witness declares that when a soldier had fired his pistol and then threw the now useless weapon at an enemy's face it could not fall afterwards to the ground, but lay on a platform of interlocked spears. Such fighting was more strenuous than deadly. The opponents were too closely jammed together for their unwieldy pikes to be of much avail.

Gradually, by reason of their position on the higher ground, the regent's men got the upper hand, and drove the others down the hill. A charge by the Macfarlanes, claymore in hand, is said to have been the closing incident of the battle. Before the onrush of the High-landers the last resolute party of Mary's army broke and scattered. Then the pursuit began. It did not last for long. To Moray's honour it must be remembered that he refused to shed a drop more than needed to be of the blood of his countrymen, his enemies though they were. The regent had given the strictest orders that, when victory had been gained, there was to be an end of killing, and he was faithfully obeyed.

The battle of Langside lasted only three-quarters of an hour. Of Mary's troops between two and three hundred were slain, almost all of them by the hagbutters behind the hedges; the regent lost only a few. Compared to any of the great battles in Scottish history, the engagement was no more than a skirmish; yet, for the time, it settled the destiny of Scotland. It established the Reformed religion, put an end to the French alliance, and shattered the last hopes of Mary Stewart.

From the "Court Knowe" at Cathcart, still marked by a stone, the queen had watched the battle. When it became known beyond doubt that all was lost, she fled southward, to make her way to England, to the false promises of her jealous cousin Elizabeth, to long years of imprisonment and to her death on the scaffold at the hands of the treacherous English queen.

GLENLIVET (3rd October, 1594).—Towards the end of 1592, it was discovered that certain of the Catholic nobility of Scotland were in treasonable correspondence with the king of Spain. The affair was glossed over; but other offences followed, and, by the autumn of 1594, the Catholic districts of the north were practically in open rebellion, led by the earls of Huntly and Errol. The earl of Argyll was sent with an army, chiefly of his own clansmen and dependants, to restore the authority of the king. At Glenlivet, in Banffshire, he encountered the rebels, who inflicted on him a severe defeat. A stronger government force, however, under the young duke of Lennox, succeeded shortly afterwards in restoring order in the north.

The Wars of Montrose — Covenanter and Royalist

BRIDGE OF DEE;	18th-19th June, 1639.
TIPPERMUIR;	1st September, 1644.
ABERDEEN;	13th September, 1644.
FYVIE;	28th October, 1644.
INVERLOCHY;	2nd February, 1645.
DUNDEE;	4th April, 1645.
AULDEARN;	9th May, 1645.
ALFORD;	2nd July, 1645.
KILSYTH;	15th August, 1645.
PHILIPHAUGH;	13th September, 1645.
CARBISDALE;	27th April, 1650.

FEW of the figures that move across the pages of Scottish history have aroused such controversy as the bitter arguments which have for their centre James Graham, first marquis of Montrose. He was a Covenanter, and he was a royalist; he fought against the king, and for the king. The conclusion to be most readily assumed from such a story is that he was a turncoat and a traitor. Yet a little reflection, after even a brief study of the facts, will surely shew that, whatever may have been Montrose's attitude to the contending powers of his day, in one thing he was always faithful, his devotion to his own conception of right and justice.

When the General Assembly met in the nave of Saint Mungo's Cathedral in 1638, to depose the bishops of Scotland, Montrose, as an elder of the church, was one of its members, and he was amongst the foremost in denunciation of the over-stepping by the king of his royal prerogative. When, in later years, the position was altered, and the people had become the oppressors, he was equally opposed to this new injustice. His voice and his sword were ever ready in the cause of

THE WARS OF MONTROSE

liberty; tyranny he would not countenance, no matter
who the tyrant might be.

The Assembly of 1638 represented the mass of the
people and the nobility of Scotland. There were some,
however, of each class who still held by the king and his
bishops. Of those the most powerful were in the north,
where the Gordons held sway. That numerous and
warlike clan had never been particularly amenable to
dictation by kings or parliaments, and in the fastnesses
of the uplands of Aberdeenshire and Banffshire they
were strong enough to hold themselves almost independent of either. Those of them who did not cling
still to the Roman faith had become staunchly episcopal.
Presbyterianism they abhorred to a man, and they had
both the will and the power to make themselves dangerous
enemies to the General Assembly.

To Montrose was allotted the task of dealing with them.
He was then twenty-seven years of age.

Early in 1639 the young general set about the raising
of his troops in his own countryside of Angus, and
arranged for the Covenanters of the north, the Frasers,
Keiths, Crichtons and Forbeses, to meet him in arms at
Turriff. The Gordons, whose chief was the marquis of
Huntly, were not long in hearing of these warlike preparations. They assembled to the number of two
thousand men, with the idea of forestalling their
enemies; but, quickly as they gathered, and Gordons
were never laggards in war, they were not quick enough
for Montrose. With two hundred horsemen he made a
forced march through the Grampians to Turriff, where
he was joined by eight hundred of his allies. When
Huntly arrived at the town, it was to find the walls
of the churchyard lined with Covenanting muskets;
so he drew off his force again and fell back on Aberdeen
in the hope of fortifying and holding that city.

Here Montrose was before him once more. With an
army now strongly reinforced by the arrival of his main
body from the south, he rode into Aberdeen on the 30th

of March, imposed a fine on the corporation, and went off again in search of Huntly.

There was much marching and counter-marching, and a good deal of somewhat questionable diplomacy, in the course of which Huntly gave himself, on promise of safe conduct, into the hands of the Covenant. The king had raised an army in England and marched it to the south side of the Border, where it was faced by a Scottish force under Alexander Leslie. The two glowered at each other for several weeks, neither of them particularly anxious for a battle, and eventually an arrangement was come to, in the middle of June, by which the General Assembly was to be considered supreme in all ecclesiastical affairs and the king in all civil.

While events were thus moving slowly towards peace in the south, the more fiery royalists of the north had been active. On the 5th of June two of Huntly's sons, Lord Aboyne and Lord Lewis Gordon, the latter a precocious warrior of thirteen, entered Aberdeen at the head of a thousand of their clansmen. They were quickly joined by more of the king's men, Ogilvies, Urquharts and Setons. The burghers, too, faithful to their tradition of loyalty to the royal house, were not slow in arming themselves for its defence. Within a week Aboyne was in command of four thousand men.

Montrose was at Stonehaven, where his troops had been joined by those of the Earl Marischal, the leading Covenanter of the north-east, whose castle of Dunnottar was one of the most powerful fortresses in Scotland.

Aboyne had seemingly decided that the force at his command justified his assuming the offensive. He marched his men into the Mearns, with the ambitious object presumably of attacking Dunnottar. On the 15th of June he reached Megray Hill near Stonehaven. There he encountered the Covenanters, and under the raking fire of their artillery his Highlanders broke and fled for the hills, their ardour for the king quite satisfied by the loot which they had collected from the estate of his

enemy, the Earl Marischal. With what remained of
his army, the best part of his own Gordons and the
burghers of Aberdeen, the royalist leader retreated
northwards, to make a stand at the Bridge of Dee. It
was a strong and well chosen position. The river was in
full flood, and the bridge was narrow. By resolute men
it could be held with little difficulty against a force
far superior in numbers.

Following close on the heels of Aboyne came Montrose.
His invariable rule, and often the secret of his success,
through all his campaigns was speed. He drew up his
troops on a slope overlooking the bridge, and, on the
morning of the 18th of June, opened fire on the earthworks which had been hastily thrown up by the defenders.
All that day the cannon and muskets of the Covenanters
showered iron and lead on their foes; but nightfall
found the royalists full of spirit and but little injured by
the bombardment they had suffered.

During the night Montrose had his heavier artillery
brought from Stonehaven. At daybreak he made a
diversion by sending his cavalry up the river towards a
ford which his opponents should have known was no
danger to them for it was impassable through the flood.
They fell into the trap, however, drawing off a large
body of their horsemen to meet this new apparent
threat. Then Montrose, after a salvo with the full
strength of his artillery, sent his footmen at the bridge.
The weakened defence crumbled up before the attack.
The Gordons made off to their own territory, taking their
chief, against his will, along with them. For a little
the citizens of Aberdeen held out alone against odds that
now were overwhelming. Then they too broke and
fled.

Most of the leaders of the Covenanters were for
summary vengeance on the defiant northern city. They
demanded that it should be given over to pillage. But
Montrose would have none of it, so the townsmen
escaped with a fine of 7000 merks.

K

As we have seen, a peace was patched up between the
king and his presbyterian subjects, the treaty being
actually signed on the day before the storming of the
Bridge of Dee. It did not last for long. Having
secured its own liberty, the General Assembly sought to
encroach on that of the king and of those who thought
with him in matters of religion. In England also, the
dispute between Charles I and his people was drawing
towards a crisis. Armies were raised by both sides,
Cromwell appeared on the scene, and the Civil War
began in the summer of 1644.

As the writer in the *Dictionary of National Biography*
puts it: "Montrose saw in the political predominance
of the presbyterian clergy all that he had detested in
the political predominance of the bishops." His duty
appeared clear to him. He offered his sword to the
king.

In April, 1644, he received his commission as lieutenant
general of the royal forces in Scotland. In August he
was in Perth, raising his army, as so often a general had
to do in those days. He had considerable success among
the clans of the central Highlands. For them it was
enough that Argyll and the Campbells were for Presbytery and Parliament; the hereditary foes of the sons of
Diarmaid must take up the cause of the king. The
Gordons and their allies in the north-east were more
slow to be roused; they had memories of the Bridge of
Dee. That was a disappointment, but the place of
those useful fighters was taken by a considerable body of
men from the north of Ireland, most of them of Scottish
blood, Macdonalds and Macleods, led by a Highland
chieftain, Alasdair Macdonald of Islay, usually incorrectly
referred to by the name of his father, Colkitto.

Alasdair was a man of mighty strength and fearless
courage. He had no skill in strategy, and was much
given to drink. In short, he was probably as Sir James
Turner described him, "no sojer, though stout enough."
But he had a genius for inspiring men with a share of his

own desperate bravery.   He was a born leader, and he is
entitled to his share of the credit of the astonishing
campaign in which he played so prominent a part.
Montrose provided the brain, Alasdair Macdonald fired
the spirit of the army; between them they wrought what
must be regarded as almost a military miracle.

The army with which they embarked on their adventure
had little to commend it to a general, beyond the natural
courage of the man in its ranks.   There were some 2200
of them in all.   Alasdair had a following of 1100; the
Atholl clans, Stewarts and Robertsons, brought 800 into
the field; and there were 300 men from Badenoch,
Macdonalds and a few Gordons.   For cavalry, there
were exactly three horses, miserable screws about ready
for the knacker.   There was no artillery, not so much as a
single field-gun, and in the treasury chest there was not a
single shilling.   A few of the better class of the men
were armed with flintlocks, others had matchlocks, very
ancient and almost useless, a greater number carried bows
and arrows, of pikes and claymores there was a fair
supply, but many had no more deadly weapons than
cudgels of oak or thorn.   One thing, however, all of
them had in plenty, the iron physique of the Highlander,
unwearying in travel, hardened to exposure and want.

Practically the whole of the Scottish regular troops,
in the hands of the Covenant, were in England with the
earl of Leven, as Alexander Leslie had now become.
Those Montrose had to deal with might be described as
the second line, less accustomed to war than the regulars,
but with all the equipment necessary for an army in
the field, a plentiful supply of muskets and ammunition,
a sufficient body of cavalry and a proper transport
train.

On the 30th of August the royalists marched out of
Blair Atholl, and their tattered throng made its way
towards Perth, which had now been occupied by their
enemies.   At Buchanty they had a welcome windfall,
five hundred bowmen who had been raised by Lord

Kilpont and the Master of Maderty, by order of the Estates, to oppose Alasdair Macdonald and his kerns. When these worthies discovered that not Macdonald but Montrose, the brother-in-law of young Maderty, was in command of the army they had to meet, they most obligingly changed their coats and threw in their lot with the king.

Perth was held for the Covenant by Lord Elcho, with 7000 footmen, 700 horse and nine pieces of ordnance, besides ample ammunition and supplies. His men outnumbered those of Montrose by about three to one, so they were in good heart and full of courage, cheered by the exhortations of their ministers, who, as was their wont, took the Almighty as their ally and the servant of the Covenant. "If ever," one of them declared, "God spoke certain truth out of my mouth, in His name I promise you to-day a certain victory."

Gallantly Elcho marched his host out of Perth on the morning of Sunday, the 1st of September, and drew them up in line of battle at Tippermuir, in a good position where there was room for his cavalry to operate. His ministers chose the battle cry for the day. It is interesting as an example of the blasphemy which in Covenanting mouths so often passed for religion. "Jesus and no quarter!" was the cry.

Even with the addition of the troops of Maderty and Kilpont, Montrose had barely 2700 men with whom to face the strong array of his enemies on whom he came at Tippermuir. His greatest danger was that he might be outflanked, so he was compelled to take the risk of thinning his line to only half the usual depth, in order that he might stretch it out the further. Alasdair's men were in the centre, on the right were the Atholl men, and on the left Kilpont and his bowmen.

Ever a stickler for the niceties of conduct, although in a speedy onset by his fiery Highlanders lay at the moment his greatest hope of victory, Montrose sent Maderty under a flag of truce to Elcho, bidding him remember his sworn allegiance to the king, praying him to avoid the spilling of Scottish blood, and in particular to refrain from acts of war on the Lord's day. The Covenanter seized the messenger and sent him a prisoner to Perth, promising to hang him when there was time to spare, then returned, by the hands of the drummer who had accompanied him, the answer that he had "made choice of the Lord's day for doing the Lord's will."

There was obviously nothing more to be said, so Montrose proceeded to action. He ordered his few musketeers to make ready.

The battle began with an advance by some of Elcho's cavalry. A volley from the ancient flintlocks and matchlocks sent a few harmless balls among them, but scared them so effectively that they wheeled about and made a hurried departure from the field. Then Montrose gave the word to charge, and in a moment his clansmen were surging in a wave of tartans and flashing steel towards their foes, who did not wait to meet them, but took to their heels and ran for their lives along the road to Perth.

In the battle, such as it was, less than a score of the losing side were slain. But a terrible toll was taken of them in their flight. The Highland and Irish blood was up, and it was not quickly to be cooled again. No efforts of the royal officers could keep their men from having their will of their flying enemies, whom they chased to the very gates of Perth, cutting them down as they ran, till the road for miles was strewn with their corpses. One eye-witness put it that "a man might have walked to Perth on the dead."

Montrose captured the nine guns, the baggage train, and practically the whole of the military equipment of Elcho's army, muskets, powder, balls, pikes, colours, tents and all, enough to supply every man in his own force with weapons and ammunition. The city of Perth surrendered without condition. Alasdair would fain

have sacked it, but Montrose denied him the pleasure,
contending himself with the infliction of a fine of £50
sterling and the requisition of a large supply of cloth,
so sorely needed by the Irish to cover their nakedness.
Both those impositions were met without demur. For
three days only, the royalists remained in Perth. It
was not a healthy quarter for them. At any moment
Argyll and his Campbells might appear out of the west,
and in the north Lord Burleigh had an army at Aberdeen.
Montrose had no wish to be caught between the arms of
a Covenanting nut-cracker, so he set off on his travels
again. He was prepared to meet either of his enemies
singly, but he chose the weaker one first, in the hope
probably that the news of another swift success would
put heart into those among the king's sympathisers
who still hesitated to rally to his banner, so he moved
towards Aberdeen with the intention of disposing of
Burleigh before facing Argyll.

It was a smaller army by far that marched out of
Perth on the 4th of September than had entered that
city three days before. The men from Atholl and
Badenoch, who doubtless regarded the campaign purely
as a looting expedition into the Lowlands, had mostly
secured as much booty as they could carry, so they
slunk away with it, leaving only the Irish Macdonalds
to follow the captured drums that now were beating for
Montrose. The whole column would amount perhaps
to 1500 men.

On the 12th of September, the Estates issued a proclamation that was typical of the regard for the usages of
civilised warfare held by those who were fighting for
Christ's Crown and Covenant. To anyone who would
kill Montrose, and bring his head to Edinburgh for
evidence, they offered a reward of £1600 sterling and a
general absolution for any crimes of which he might have
been guilty in the past.

That same day, the royalists arrived in sight of Aberdeen. Contrary to their hopes, they had raised but few

recruits by the way, the only notable accession to their strength being the earl of Airlie with forty-five horsemen, and Nathaniel Gordon of Ardlogie with thirty. The Gordon clan at the moment was strangely divided against itself. The marquis was holding himself aloof at Strathnaver, his second son, Aboyne, was with the king's men at Carlisle, while the other two, Lord Gordon and Lord Lewis Gordon, were actually with Burleigh's Covenanting force in Aberdeen. A portion of the clan was with each of them.

Montrose found his enemies strongly posted on a hillside, at the foot of which were a number of houses and gardens, forming an excellent shelter for the advanced line of defenders. The others were established in a good position on the slope. Their infantry were two thousand strong, their cavalry five hundred.

On the morning of the 13th, Montrose sent a message to the magistrates of Aberdeen, informing them that he was "there for the maintenance of religion and liberty and his Majesty's just authority and service," and demanding the immediate surrender of the city, following with a threat that, if his orders were not complied with, no mercy would be shewn to the burghers. It was quaintly subscribed, " I am, as you deserve, Montrose."

A manly answer was sent back to him. The townsmen protested that they had "been ever known to be most loyal and dutiful subjects to his Majesty," and hoped "by God's grace to strive to continue so;" but declared that they could not so lightly surrender their city as he desired, for they had been guilty of no offence against either religion, liberty, or the king.

The officer who had brought the original ultimatum into the town and the drummer boy who accompanied him were civilly entertained and the boy was given a piece of money. Then, under a flag of truce, they set off with their reply. As they passed Burleigh's lines, the drummer was shot dead, a foolish act of treachery for which the unfortunate city of Aberdeen, quite guiltless of it, was to pay dearly.

The battle was begun by Alaisdair Macdonald's caterans. They threw themselves upon the houses and gardens at the foot of the hill, and found little difficulty in clearing out the defenders. Then they began to push their way up the slope.

From Burleigh's left Lord Lewis Gordon rode forward with a few horsemen, in a feint attack which was no more than a display of bravado intended to cover a more serious effort on the other flank. There, out of sight in a sunk road, a party of 400 foot and 100 horse made their way round Montrose's left, and, had they been more resolute fighters than they were, might easily have opened the way to victory for the Covenant. As it was, Nathaniel Gordon, with his thirty horsemen and a few musketeers, brushed them harmlessly aside. Some riders from the other flank came to Gordon's support, and he led a dashing counter-attack that completely routed the detachment of Covenanters.

Sir William Forbes of Craigievar, one of Burleigh's cavalry leaders, observing that Montrose's right flank had been weakened by the loss of the party which had gone to Gordon's assistance, gave his horsemen the order to charge. He led them down the hill in a headlong gallop, a furious rush before which most lines of infantry might have crumpled and broken. But Alasdair's men very coolly awaited their coming, opened their ranks and allowed the horses to pass through them, then swung round and emptied their muskets into the ranks of the horsemen. In a moment the gallant charge had become the flight of a panic-stricken rabble.

Burleigh's cavalry was gone; his footmen were at the mercy of the grim fighters who opposed them. Montrose gave the order to advance, and his whole line swept up the hill, claymore in hand. The Covenanters made little effort at resistance; raw levies, they had not much stomach for an encounter with the fierce swordsmen who came rushing on them.

It had ceased to be a battle now, and soon became a rout, the men of the Covenant flying for the shelter of Aberdeen, their enemies close behind them, hewing and hacking with relentless steel. It was Tippermuir over again. And worse than Tippermuir. At Perth, Montrose had been able to keep a firm hand on his troops; here he failed, if indeed he tried. The Highlanders and Irish, drunk with victory, broke into the city, and there made little difference between the men they had defeated in the field and the peaceful burghers who were more loyal in heart to the king than were the people of almost any other town in Scotland.

What part Montrose may have played in the affair has been hotly disputed. It is almost inconceivable that he could have ordered it, in spite of the terms of his message to the magistrates; but there is no evidence that he made any attempt to stop it. The murder of his drummer boy, in which the city had no hand, has been usually advanced as the cause of the one blemish on the fair name of the Great Marquis.

During three days of bloodshed and debauch the sack of Aberdeen continued. Over a hundred of the townsfolk were slain, many women among them.

On the 16th of September, Montrose marched his men out of the city, and three days later it was entered by Argyll, who had been lumbering in the rear of the swift-footed royalists, grumbling always that the Estates grudged him a sufficient force to deal with them, in spite of the fact that he had 2500 infantry and no fewer than 1500 horsemen, twenty times the number of his opponent's little body of cavalry.

A continuous harassment to Montrose was the necessity for constant recruiting for his small army. His High-landers came and went more or less as they pleased. In an endeavour to raise some Lowlanders of less independent spirit than the Gaels, he went south, with Argyll

plodding behind him, and for weeks there was a game
to "follow the leader" from the Spey to the Tay then
back to the Don, the royalists always several days
ahead of their heavier-footed adversaries.

Ever hopeful of help from Huntly, Montrose now
moved into the Gordon country again, and Argyll
followed him.   At Fyvie, on the Ythan, they came face
to face on the 28th of October.

. Alasdair Macdonald had gone off to the west on his
own, on a recruiting expedition among his clansmen,
taking the bulk of his Irish troops with him.   This left
Montrose with no more than 800 foot and 50 horse.   Meantime Argyll's force had been augmented by the arrival
of fourteen troops of horse under the Earl Marischal.

The royal army was drawn up on the slope of a little
hill, at the foot of which the ground was broken by
ditches and dry-stone dykes.   Behind them was a
wood, which they counted on to defend them from Argyll's
overpowering force of cavalry.   They had little ammunition, little indeed of anything from which to hope for
victory save their own unwavering courage.

The Covenanters began the battle, one of their regiments advancing with considerable spirit, and quickly
succeeding in driving the royalists back from the dykes
and ditches at the foot of the hill.   Montrose was in
desperate straits; he seemed to be trapped at last.   But
he was as unruffled as ever, and so, apparently, were his
men.   To a young Ulsterman named O'Kean, one of
Alasdair's lieutenants, a man known to be without the
knowledge of fear, he gave the task of driving the
Covenanters with cold steel out of their newly won
position.   The Irishman did not hesitate for a moment.
Collecting a handful of men of like spirit to his own,
he rushed with them down the hillside, and their enemies
fled almost before they were on them.

It was on this gallant exploit that rested the eventual
fate of the day.   From the ditches O'Kean brought
back several sacks full of precious gunpowder, abandoned

by its rightful owners, and an indignant complaint that
"the rogues have forgot to leave the bullets with the
powder." The pouches of the royal musketeers were
quickly replenished from this unexpected windfall, and
prospects looked brighter for Montrose.

Argyll's next move was to send five hundred of his
horsemen, under Lothian, to try their luck. Making
a detour round the dykes and avoiding the wood, they
attempted to take the royalists on the flank, but they
were met with a volley of musketry that sent them
reeling on the right about in complete confusion.

That ended the battle, if so ineffective a skirmish may
be distinguished by such a name. Argyll had had enough
of it for one day. His genius had always lain more
towards the argument of the council-board and the
intrigue of the closet than the more dangerous adventures
of the field. He retreated across the Ythan to a spot two
miles from the scene of the encounter, and there spent
the night under arms.

The next morning he came back again to Fyvie, and
made several faint-hearted attempts to storm the
position, all of them miserably unsuccessful, although
the king's men were outnumbered by more than five to
one and had for ammunition only the balls they had
contrived to manufacture by melting down the pewter
tankards in Fyvie House.

On the morning of the 30th, Montrose went off un-
molested to Strathbogie, and for several days maintained
himself there against further futile attacks by Argyll.
Then he decided to retreat into the hills, so he made for
Balvenie on the Fiddich near Mortlach. There a council
of war was held. He himself was for a raid on the south,
but many of the Lowland gentry among his officers did
not agree with him. They were beginning a little to
regret the loyalty which had led them to risk the safety
of their estates, and were inclined to consider the wisdom
of making their peace with the Covenant. One by one
they now slipped away to fend for themselves, Airlie,

that stout old loyalist, and his sons being almost alone in remaining true to their faith. Nathaniel Gordon went too; but there is good reason to believe that he had a very different object from the rest. He had no great estate to fear for, and he had never shewn any particular concern for his life.

With what remained to him of following, Montrose now made his way back to Blair Atholl, where he had arranged to meet Alasdair. It was a heartening company that came to him out of the west, Macdonalds of Glengarry, Clanranald and Keppoch, Stewarts of Appin, Macleans from Mull and Camerons from Lochaber. Farquharsons had come, too, from Braemar, MacIans from Glencoe, and lesser clans had sent their tale of men from far and near. Alasdair had been a good recruiter.

The devotion to the king of the Highlanders who had now flocked to his standard may not always have been beyond question, but every man of them had a grudge against the Campbells and was willing to take up any cause which gave the chance of a blow at Argyll. They were soon to have their opportunity.

Argyll had gone to Edinburgh, and returned his commission to the Estates. Then he had ridden sulkily home to Inveraray, to brood there on the shabby treatment by which he had been grudged more than four thousand men to deal with Montrose and his desperate eight hundred. He had had enough of the empty charms of war. Among his own people he would be well away from it.

Montrose had other views on the subject. The most useful purpose he could see for himself at the moment was to put completely out of action the greatest of the Covenanting nobles, and he knew that in no other endeavour could he look to his men to give a better account of themselves. So he resolved on a raid into Lorn.

Argyll was not without good enough reason in his

belief that in his own territory he was free from any
threat of war.   The Campbell country, fertile and
civilised in comparison to the wild Highlands which lay
to the north and east of it, was almost a little kingdom by
itself.   Inveraray, on the shore of Loch Fyne, was like a
Lowland town, with its shops, its ministers, and its
prosperous merchants who carried on an extensive
trade by sea with the south and the Continent.   Far
spread around it were lush glens with great herds of
cattle, and beyond them was a wall of mountains through
which only a few narrow passes gave access to the lands of
Lorn.   A handful of resolute men at each of those danger
points might suffice to ward off an army of enemies.

Montrose chose to attempt none of those recognised
gateways, but, with astonishing audacity, plunged into
the heart of the hills, struggled over trackless bogs, crossed
mountain torrents and penetrated glens that few but
he would ever have thought possible for the passage of
an army.   Presently he found himself on the shores of
Loch Awe, and it was but a short step from there to
Loch Fyne and Inveraray.

Argyll was suddenly roused from his dream of security
by the astounding news that his enemy was coming
down Glen Shira with an army at his tail.   Always
swift of action when his own skin was in peril, he
scrambled on board a fishing boat and sped down the loch
towards the shelter of his castle of Roseneath, which he
reckoned was near enough to the fortress of Dunbarton
to give him an assurance of safety.

Montrose and his Highlanders entered Inveraray
almost without opposition, and there they lived on the
fat of the land for a couple of months.   There was little
killing, though now and again an obstreperous Campbell
may have called for a dirking; but there was feasting
such as the lean clansmen had never thought to find on
this side of heaven, beef and bread galore, and wine in
plenty to wash them down.

At Roseneath Argyll had been squealing like a rat in

a corner, calling on the Estates to come to his aid. He
was a poor type of a son of Diarmaid, for, whatever
may be urged against them on other scores, his clan had
never been unhandy with the sword. Had their chief
but taken the field with them, he could have fended well
enough for himself against the raiders. As it was, he
waited at Roseneath until the arrival of sixteen companies
of militia. Then he summoned his clan. But he had
done with soldiering himself; he gave the command to his
kinsman, Sir Duncan Campbell of Auchinbreck.

The Estates had now awakened to the full seriousness
of the threat which Montrose was making against their
authority. A considerable force of regulars, under
Baillie of Letham, was assembled at Perth to help to deal
with him, and in the north the earl of Seaforth was bidden
to collect an army among the friends of the Covenant
there.

Once again Montrose seemed to be in a trap. By
January Argyll had three thousand men and Seaforth
five thousand. The former were the most to be feared;
they were good fighting men, all of them. Although
Seaforth was nominally the head of the Mackenzies,
he was far from representing the political views of his
powerful clan. Few of them joined him, and his army
consisted for the most part, as described by a contemporary, of "a mere rabble of new levies, peasants, drovers,
shopmen, servants and camp-followers."

To remain at Inveraray would now have proved fatal
for the royalists, so by the latter days of January, 1645,
they were on the march again. They went by Loch Awe
and Loch Etive, then by Appin into Glencoe, through the
comparative safety of Lochaber, and on to Kilcumin at
the head of Loch Ness. There, on the 29th, their spies
brought them definite word of the whereabouts of their
foes. Seaforth was at Inverness, and the Campbells at
Inverlochy. Montrose decided to dispose of the latter
first, a hardy resolution with fifteen hundred men against
their three thousand.

On the morning of the 31st of January the little army set off on its desperate adventure, to accomplish a feat that is without parallel in the history of warfare in Britain. It was bitter wintry weather, the passes almost blocked with drifting snow, the ground ice-bound beneath their ill-shod feet, a piercing wind chilling them to the bone as they fought their way through the heart of the hills. And to add to their suffering, their only food for officers and men alike was a little oatmeal moistened with icy water.

All through that day, and all through the night, they struggled forward, their limbs stiffened by the cold, their eyes blinded by the wind, their bodies aching with weariness and hunger. By the side of his men walked their leader, taking his share with them of all the hardships of the march. There was never a halt; the man who lay down in that frozen wilderness stood little chance of ever rising again.

On the morning of the 1st of February they were at Roy Bridge. Inverlochy was thirteen miles away by the shortest road, but Montrose had no thought of going that way. He meant to take Argyll by surprise so he made a detour among the hills, and by nightfall was looking down on the camp of the Campbells at Inverlochy. There, on the frozen ground, without food or fire, their scanty clothing soaked by melted snow and the water of the streams they had forded, the royal army passed the night.

They had been seen by Argyll's outposts, but no great thought was given to them, for it seemed clearly impossible that more than a scouting party could have made its way from Roy Bridge, where Montrose was known to have been two days before. Argyll was a man, however, who took every personal precaution. Even a small body of raiders might do considerable mischief in a night attack, so MacCailean Mor took to the waters again, embarking on a galley which was anchored in the middle of the loch. At daybreak he was astounded by the salute to the royal standard on Montrose's trumpets.

There was wild excitement in the camp and a hurried scrambling to arms. Auchinbreck formed his line with the Campbells in the centre and the Lowland regiments on the wings. Facing them, Montrose himself commanded the centre, composed of his Highlanders, and on the flanks were the Irish under Alasdair and O'Kean.

It was those two gallant soldiers of fortune who opened the battle with a wild dash by their Ulstermen against the militia. The Lowlanders made no effort to stand, but took to their heels and fled. Then Montrose advanced with his main body. Deserted and outflanked as they now were, the Campbells fought bravely for a while. As a royalist chronicler put it, "they were stout and gallant men, worthy of a better chief and a juster cause." But gradually they were forced back. Then they broke and scattered.

Then began the pursuit and the scenes of blood that as usual went with it. The Lowland men were given quarter; but there could be no mercy from Macdonalds or Macleans or Stewarts towards their hereditary foes. For miles the shores of Loch Lochy and Loch Eil were strewn with the bodies of Campbells, fifteen hundred of them, as many as the whole force of the victors. Meanwhile the galley of Argyll was speeding rapidly down the loch towards the sea and Roseneath.

If Inverlochy had no other lasting result, it had destroyed the fighting power of the Campbells for ever. The house of Argyll was to remain powerful, but it was no longer to be by the claymore.

Montrose was anxious now to make at last a descent on the Lowlands, but without cavalry this could have no chance of success. The only hope he had of obtaining horsemen was among the Gordon gentry in the north, so there he went. He was not disappointed. Nathaniel Gordon's desertion to the opposing camp had served its purpose. He had won his clan away from the Covenant,

and now came back to Montrose with Lord Gordon,
Huntly's heir, and two hundred well-mounted men.
There were other recruits also, notably three hundred
Grants; and even Seaforth came to make his peace. He
had been temporarily a Covenanter only because the
Macdonalds were royalists.

Happy in the brighter prospect that seemed to lie
before him, Montrose moved with his army southward
down the east coast, burning as they went an occasional
house of some stubborn Covenanter who refused to
meet the demands that were made on him. General
Baillie's army, although considerably superior in numbers
and especially in cavalry, kept determinedly out of his
way.

On the 4th of April he came to Dundee. That town
had long annoyed him by its opposition to the king's
cause, and now seemed the fitting occasion to teach it a
lesson. It was a small place, but it was well garrisoned
by volunteers and protected by a strong wall, behind
which were mounted several pieces of artillery. A
message was sent to the magistrates, demanding the
keys. They were slow in replying, so a breach was made
in the wall at a point where it was being repaired. The
garrison discreetly retired, and the royalists poured into
the town, to commence at once a glorious spree on the
wine and spirits with which the warehouses were well
filled. By afternoon scarcely a man was sober among
them; and at the height of their debauch came word
that Baillie's troops were approaching. It looked as if
Montrose's hour had come, but, in one of the most
marvellous achievements of his whole astonishing career,
he collected his drunken caterans and bundled them out
of the town by the East Port as Baillie's vanguard came
in by the West. All through the night they marched,
sobered by their peril, fighting rear-guard actions as
they went, and by morning they were safe among the
hills where Baillie's horsemen could not follow them.

Montrose's enemies were now mustering fast, and it

L

became increasingly necessary to beat up more recruits for the king. Alasdair went off to the west again, and Lord Gordon rode to the north to rouse his clan, while Montrose more slowly followed him. At Skene, about 10 miles from Aberdeen, they reassembled. Alasdair had had some success, and Gordon had raised 1000 foot and 200 horse.

The Covenanting general in the north was a man named Hurry, a soldier of fortune who had once been a royalist and was to be one again. He had four regiments of regular infantry with him, and all the clans who hated the Gordons—-Frasers, Forbeses, Roses and the like— between 4000 and 5000 men in all, of whom five hundred were mounted. With this force he set off towards the west, after raiding the Gordon country, and Montrose followed him. On the morning of the 9th of May they came to battle at the little village of Auldearn, not far from Nairn.

Hurry had turned during the night, in the hope of taking his enemies by surprise. He almost succeeded, and it was little time Montrose had in the grey light of the early morning to make his dispositions. The village lay on the slope of a ridge. At the north end of it was placed Alasdair with a mixed body of Irish and Gordons. A few men were distributed among the houses, and the main body, including the cavalry, were concealed on the other side of the ridge. In front of Alasdair there was only a narrow strip of firm ground; the rest was bog.

Hurry fell into the trap so cleverly prepared for him, but he was almost saved from it by Alasdair's rash impetuosity. The reckless Macdonald was never a man to wait patiently for an enemy to come at him. While the Covenanting regiments were making their way past the bog, he rushed forward to meet them, regardless of the fact that his five hundred men were outnumbered by eight to one. Against untrained levies such as he had met before he might have succeeded, but the men who faced him now were among the best in the Scottish regular army. There was no panic for them, and, stoutly as the Irish and the Gordons fought, they were overwhelmed and forced back on the village, fighting like madmen among the houses and pig-styes.

Now or never Montrose must launch his counter-attack. He did not hesitate. The Gordon horsemen came out of their concealment, and charged with the cry of "Strathbogie!" The irregular cavalry who were on Hurry's right wing fled at the sight of them, leaving the flank of their infantry exposed to all the force of the Gordon hurricane of horses and steel. Then Montrose brought his reserves over the crest of the hill, and threw them into the fight. The Frasers and Forbeses went off without striking a blow, and the four regular regiments were doomed. They fought desperately, but in the end they were broken.

There was a pursuit that lasted for fourteen miles. In it and in the battle Hurry's army is reckoned to have had 2000 men slain. The general himself escaped, though, like the stout soldier that he was, he was one of the last to leave the field.

Hurry's force had been destroyed, but there was still another Covenanting army in the field. Baillie, with 2000 foot and 500 horse, had come north, and was harrying Strathbogie in revenge for the exploits of the Gordons. Montrose must dispose of him too, but first he had as usual to raise the necessary troops, for most of his western Highlanders had gone off with their booty from Auldearn, leaving him but few more than the Gordons and the Irish. Alasdair, with part of his Ulstermen for bodyguard, went to rally the Macdonalds again, while Montrose led Baillie a dance between the Spey, the Dee and the Don, biding a favourable chance to give him battle. It came at Alford on the Don, on the 2nd of July. Alasdair had not returned, but some hundreds of Baillie's footmen had been withdrawn from him by the Estates, so there was now no great disparity in infantry between the two forces. In cavalry, however, the Gordon horsemen were out-numbered by their opponents by two to one.

Montrose had established himself, after his usual manner, on a stretch of rising ground, protected in front by the river and a bog. In the centre of his front line he had his Highlanders, Gordons, Farquharsons and Badenoch men. On the flanks were the cavalry, stiffened with Irish musketeers, and carefully hidden behind the hill was the reserve, the greater part of the infantry.

Baillie forded the river, and skirted the bog. Then Lord Gordon, who commanded the cavalry on the royalist right, gave the order to his men to charge. They came thundering down on the Covenanters' left, where the infantry immediately broke. Three squadrons of horsemen, however, commanded by Balcarres, stood their ground, and joined with the Gordons in a fierce cavalry fight, horse to horse and sword to sword. For a space the rest of the two armies watched this encounter as mere spectators. Then Nathaniel Gordon led his dismounted clansmen into the battle. They could not shoot, for fear of injuring their own men, so they threw down their muskets, and with their claymores set about houghing the Covenanters' horses. That finished Balcarres's cavalry. The survivors of them were glad to escape with their lives. On the other flank, Lord Aboyne had charged and broken the wing that faced him, and all that was needed to complete the victory was the advance of Montrose's reserve. The Covenanters were outflanked and outfought. Soon they were in full flight across the Howe of Alford, with their exultant enemies raging after them.

At Alford Baillie lost as many men as Hurry had done at Auldearn. The royalist losses were few, but there was one which seemed to many to have turned the victory almost into a defeat. While pressing ahead of his men in a reckless effort to capture Baillie, the young Lord Gordon was shot dead. He is described by John Buchan as "the one man who in temper and attainments was fitted to be the companion of Montrose."

At Naseby, on the 14th June, Cromwell had inflicted a crushing blow on the king's forces in England, and it became increasingly apparent to Montrose that, however many armies he might overthrow in the north, his achievements there could be of no lasting value to the cause he served. It was in the south that the war would be lost and won. The time had come when he must put his fate to the touch, so, leaving Aboyne to follow him with Gordon reinforcements, he began his southward march.

At Fordoun he was met by Alasdair, with his Ulstermen and 1000 Highlanders, almost half of them from the fighting clan of Maclean. At Dunkeld Aboyne rejoined, bringing with him 200 cavalry and 120 mounted infantry. Montrose was now in command of an army of about 4500 foot and 500 horse, the most powerful force he had ever had at his disposal.

The Scottish parliament was thoroughly alarmed. Orders were given for the levying immediately of 10,000 more infantry and 500 cavalry, and Baillie, who twice within a few weeks resigned his commission in disgust at the interference of the committee with which he was saddled, was persuaded to remain in command.

Until the middle of August the two armies marched about the skirts of the Highlands, playing for position and biding their time. On the 15th of that month they found themselves face to face at Kilsyth. Baillie had 6000 foot and 800 horse. And he had a committee, which included such doughty warriors as Argyll, Elcho, Burleigh and Balcarres, all with the sting of Montrose still burning in their hides. These four, as the unfortunate general well knew, were more than enough to deprive him of any advantage his superior numerical strength might have given him.

Montrose's men had spent the night encamped in a meadow at the foot of the Campsies. In the morning they discovered the Covenanters on the ridge of a hill above them. It was not like Montrose to leave unoccupied ground higher than his own; but this time he may have done it for a bait. In any case, there was no very great danger in it, for the hillside and the boggy ground around the burn at the foot of it were impossible for cavalry.

Baillie was wary; he felt that a trap might have been laid for him, and was content to wait in his strong position on the hill. Not so, however, his precious committee. They saw the sweet balm of revenge waiting to soothe the wounds Montrose had given them, and they were all impatience. Their enemy was within their grasp at last; they must get at him before he could slip off to the Highlands again. To leave him no chance of escape, they would occupy the hill, on his left flank, which lay between him and the north, and attack him from there.

Baillie was horrified by the suggestion, for to get to the new position meant marching across Montrose's front, a foolishly dangerous manoeuvre. His protests were brushed aside, and the march began. In the van went Balcarres with the mounted men, and the infantry followed. There seems to have been no attempt made at concealment.

What Montrose's plan of action may have been can never be known, for the battle was taken suddenly out of his hands. In the glen, where the burn ran between the two hills, there were a few cottages held by a party of a hundred Macleans. About half the Covenanters had passed, when a small body of them detached themselves and made an attack on the cottages. They were easily repulsed by the garrison, and were footing it up the hillside again, when Alasdair, never able to resist a challenge, broke away from Montrose's line with some of his Macdonalds and went after them.

It was too much, of course, to expect that the rest of the Highlanders would stand meekly by and watch the chase. In an instant the bulk of them were racing up the glen and the hillside, making straight for the centre of the enemy's column. Four regiments of the Covenanting foot took up a hasty position behind a dyke on the ridge of the hill, but their shelter was of little avail to them. The clansmen leapt over the wall, swords in hand, scattered their opponents, and in a few moments had cut the Covenant's army in two.

Now the Gordon cavalry, with Airlie's troopers to back them, came into the fight. They attacked Balcarres's horsemen, who at first put up a stout resistance but soon were overborne and driven from the field.

There remained now only Baillie's rear, made up of levies from Fife. The general made a desperate effort to rally them, but they had their own views on the matter and quietly departed by the shortest route for home.

The inevitable murderous pursuit followed the battle of Kilsyth. As was usual in the case of a defeat of a Covenanting army, the victims were confined to the common men; their leaders, on swifter horses, knew how to look to the safety of their own skins. Baillie did his utmost to save the battle; but the others left early, and some of them carried their caution to an extreme that was almost ludicrous. Loudon and Lindsay fled to England. Glencairn and Cassillis did not feel safe till they had reached the shores of Ireland. Argyll also, as was his custom, took to the water. He rode to Queensferry, and there got a boat which carried him to Berwick.

If only the king had had in England a leader fit to be compared with Montrose, and men the match of Alasdair's Highlanders, he would not have lost his head or even his throne. As it was, the English royalists never recovered from the staggering blow they had been dealt at Naseby. They struggled on in a desultory campaign, but they had no chance of success. With a competent general and a fighting army, they would have

joined hands with the man who had now cleared Scotland
of the king's enemies, and the whole subsequent course of
British history would have been altered.

After Kilsyth Montrose set about consolidating his
victory. All the towns in the south surrendered to him.
Glasgow, indeed, which had had no Covenanting fanatic-
ism, made him welcome, and Edinburgh excused herself
by pleading that she had been forced into rebellion by a
few malcontents. All the royalist prisoners in Edinburgh
tolbooth, and it was packed full of them, were liberated.
The castle of that city, however, was still in the hands
of the Covenant, and there Montrose's heir, the young
Lord Graham, was held captive. He was offered an
exchange, and the gallant boy refused it, saying that
the liberty of one so young and of so little use in the field
was not worth his father's sacrifice of a single enemy
prisoner.

Montrose had great hopes of the Border barons with
their moss-troopers, and it looked as if he was not to be
disappointed in them. The earls of Home and Roxburgh
promised their aid. Better still, the marquis of Douglas
threw in his lot with the king, and undertook to raise
the tenants on his vast estates in Clydesdale.

A parliament was summoned to meet in Glasgow on
the 20th of October, "for settling religion and peace,"
and by the early days of September Montrose felt himself
ready to begin his march to the south. Most of his
strength lay in promises, for in actual numbers of men
he had probably a smaller force than any he had commanded since Tippermuir. The western Highlanders
had no great love for the thought of regular warfare in
the Lowlands, far removed from their own homes, and in
any case their enemy was not the Covenant but the
marquis of Argyll. In this Alasdair was inclined to agree
with them, so, with the Macdonalds, the Macleans
and the Appin men, and half of the Irish, he went off
on a private campaign of his own into Kintyre. Five
hundred Ulstermen, under the faithful O'Kean, decided

to stand by Montrose. On the 4th of September the
little royalist army set out from Bothwell on its march
to the Tweed, and by night it had suffered a loss even
greater than that of Alasdair and his Highlanders. The
touchy Gordon blood of Aboyne was roused by what he
felt to be a slight when the command of the cavalry was
given to another, and in a dudgeon he rode off with the
whole of his clansmen, horse and foot. Old Nathaniel
was the only one of his following who refused to go with
him.

Two days later Montrose was at Cranstoun, near
Dalkeith. There he got news that must have been
alarming in view of the now depleted state of his army.
David Leslie, the greatest general the Covenant ever had,
brilliant and ruthless, was marching north to intercept
him with a force of 6000 men, more than 5000 of them
well-mounted cavalry. Leslie had been with the troops
that were besieging Hereford, and should never have
been allowed by the English royalists to reach the Border.
He himself admitted that if they had attacked him on
the way, with the force which he knew to be at their
command, they would have cut his column to pieces.
They were probably glad enough, however, to see what
they hoped to be the last of him, and on the 6th of
September he crossed the Tweed.

That day Montrose was marching down Gala Water.
At Torwoodlee, on the 7th, he was joined by Douglas
with a body of horse, lairds and lairds' sons most of them,
from Clydesdale and Nithsdale. They had never smelt
powder and had no great ambition to, but they were
very welcome, poor substitutes though they were for the
Gordon riders who had gone off.

On the 9th, Montrose was at Kelso, the meeting place
with Home and Roxburgh. There was not a trooper
awaiting him. Instead, there was the news that the
two earls were prisoners of Leslie, not unwilling captives
if local rumour might be believed.

The royalists moved further up the Tweed, still in the

hope of rousing the Border clans. On the afternoon of the 12th they were at Philiphaugh, a piece of level ground lying below Selkirk. There they decided to camp. It was a strong position; behind them was a hill, and the other three sides were protected by the Ettrick and the Yarrow. Some earthworks were thrown up, and a patrol was sent out; then the troops settled down for the night. Montrose had a lodging in Selkirk.

Late that night Leslie arrived at the little village of Sunderland, three miles away. There was a royalist picket there, which retired after the exchange of a few musket shots, and fell back on Philiphaugh with their news of the enemy. They were not believed.

At daybreak on the 13th a dense autumn mist lay over the haugh. The sentries could not see three yards in front of them. The men in the camp were finishing their morning meal, and through the mist there crept towards them two thousand of Leslie's horsemen who had forded the Ettrick during the night. The damp white shroud that lay around all the countryside smothered even the beat of the horses' hoofs and the rattle of their bridles as the dragoons rode into position. When it began to thin with the rising sun, they were already within striking distance. James Agnew of Lochnaw was at the head of them. He gave the order to charge, and down on the camp they thundered.

The alarm was quickly carried to Montrose at Selkirk. He threw himself on a horse and galloped to his camp, where he found the Ulstermen and Lord Airlie's troopers fighting for their lives. Douglas's Clydesdale lairds had gone off at the sound of the first shot, leaving their leader to follow them or not as he pleased.

The Irish were fighting as they always had done, beating off charge after charge by Agnew's dragoons. Their first stand they made behind the low earthworks they had thrown up the night before; then, driven from these, they had fallen back on the dry-stone dykes around Philiphaugh farm. There they stood their ground till more than four hundred of them were slain.

Montrose put himself at the head of about a hundred horsemen he collected. They charged the enemy, then drew off, and charged again and ever again, each time taking full toll of their foes, but their own ranks thinning, too, with each gallant endeavour.

The remainder of Leslie's cavalry were on the other bank of the Ettrick. Now they, too, forded it and attacked the royalists from the flank, and soon the battle was over. Six hundred men had made a desperate effort against six thousand. To surrender now was no shame to those who were left of them, a handful of horsemen and less than a hundred Irish infantry.

By some miracle Montrose was not even wounded. His own wish would have been to die there for he would not yield, but Douglas, and others of the friends who had ridden so bravely by his side throughout the fight, persuaded him to flee for the sake of the king's cause which he still might help in the end to victory. They rode to Clydesdale, then on to the north, and shortly were safe amid the hills of Perthshire.

The fate that befell the Irish prisoners at Philiphaugh is but one of many witnesses to the fact that, whatever devotion the Covenanters may have had to the Word of God, they had but scant regard for their own. The Ulstermen surrendered on promise of their lives. Next morning they were shot down to a man in the courtyard of Newark Castle. Their followers were not spared for even so long; on the day of the battle three hundred of them, women and children, were butchered at Philiphaugh, along with two hundred unarmed men who had had no share in the fighting, cooks and horse-boys.

Of Montrose's principal officers a few escaped with him. The others were promised quarter, and surrendered. Little did they know what a slender reed was the honour of their captors on which they rested their faith. O'Kean was hanged at Edinburgh without a trial. At Glasgow, on the 20th of October, the day fixed for Montrose's parliament, some of the others were brought before a committee. Of their fate there was never a doubt. Sir William Rollo was beheaded at the Mercat Cross on the 28th, and the next day there followed him to the block Sir Philip Nisbet and Ogilvy of Inverquharity, the latter a boy in his teens. Then the scene was changed to St. Andrews that the joyous spectacle might be well distributed throughout the kingdom.

There was some delay in the trials, and the Covenanting divines began to fear that they were to be cheated of their prey. As John Buchan relates, in his history of Montrose, "the Kirk was in terror lest Parliament should be too merciful, and appeals flowed in from synods and presbyteries." A typical one which he quotes was this appeal from Dumfries: "We need not lay before your honours what the Lord calls for at your hands nor what you owe unto the many thousands of His people."

In the middle of January the Lord's people had their wish. The "Maiden" was set up, and its rusty blade fell on the loyal necks of Nathaniel Gordon, Sir Robert Spottiswoode, Andrew Guthrie, son of the bishop of Moray, and William Murray, a lad of nineteen, brother of Tullibardine.

At no time was Montrose ever long without an army. From the braes of Atholl came Robertsons and Stewarts to join him at Blair. Then he marched north, gathering Farquharsons and others as he went, and so to Speyside in the hope of bringing the Gordons back to him. In this he was partly successful, though old Huntly was a dubious ally who was more concerned with his own ends than with the king's.

Throughout the winter there was a guerilla warfare from Aberdeen to Inverness between the royalists and a little army under Middleton, one of Leslie's lieutenants. It was brought to an end by affairs in the south. The Scots fell out with their English allies and made a kind

of peace with the king.   One of the terms of the settle-
ment was that Montrose must leave Scotland.   On the
3rd of September, 1646, he sailed on a Norwegian sloop
out of the harbour of the little town to whose name he
had brought so much honour.

In the course of twelve months he had fought nine
battles and won eight of them.   He had broken and
scattered half a dozen armies.   He had been the master
of Scotland, and, with a fraction of the support which he
merited, would have kept the king on his throne.   But he
was the only general Charles I ever had.

For more than three years Montrose wandered through
the northern parts of Europe, seeking always how he
might serve his master.   He was in constant correspondence with other exiles for the cause, notably the dashing
Prince Rupert, a man after his own heart, and with the
loyalists who still remained at home.   He used every
endeavour to secure the interest of those foreign rulers
whose sympathy for the king he thought might be
turned to advantage.   His purpose was to raise a band
of mercenaries, trained fighting men, who would give a
stiffening to the army he hoped still to lead in Scotland.

On a bleak morning in January, 1649, the king was
butchered at Whitehall by the catspaws of Cromwell.
His successor, the young Charles II, was a refugee on the
Continent.   To him Montrose immediately made promise
of loyalty and service, and was appointed by him viceroy
and captain-general in Scotland.   He was not slow to
shew that he was ready to take up his office.

Better reports had been coming from the friends and
spies at home.   Most men had become thoroughly
wearied of the high-handed rule of the Covenant, and
were ready for almost any change.   Alasdair, it is true,
was gone, stabbed in the back in an obscure scuffle in
Ireland; but there were others to take his place.   Seaforth was professing loyalty; Huntly too; and the clans
of the west and the isles could always be counted on as
king's men when there was the chance of a raid into

Argyll.   Montrose was led to believe that 20,000 would
rally to his standard.

He chose Orkney as the first base for his operations.
Five hundred Danish mercenaries were sent there,
under his half-brother Harry Graham, and, in April,
1650, he followed them.   At Kirkwall he recruited 1000
Orcadians, men whose forebears had been too long at
peace for them to have any aptitude for war.   For
cavalry he had a few mounted gentlemen, not more
than fifty in all.   His hope to increase their number lay
as usual with the Gordons.

In fishing boats the tiny army crossed the Pentland
Firth on the 12th of April.   A fortnight was spent in
slowly moving southward through Caithness, where
scarcely a recruit came in.   On the 23rd they were at
Lairg, and two days later at the head of the Kyle of
Sutherland, a long, narrow inlet of the sea, where they
camped in a good position.   Behind them was the hill
of Craigcoinichean, on one flank was the Kyle and on
other a deep-running burn.   Near at hand was the little
loch of Carbisdale.   Here Montrose made the fatal
mistake of waiting for Seaforth instead of pushing
rapidly south to the Highland hills.

Hurrying to oppose him was Strachan, a subordinate
of David Leslie's.   He had only a small force, but was
well supplied with cavalry, 220 of them.

Strachan had news of Montrose's whereabouts and of
his weakness in horse.   As he came near to Carbisdale,
he concealed the greater part of his cavalry in a wood of
tall broom, and sent forward a single troop to draw on
his opponent.   The ruse was as successful as he could
have hoped it to be.

Montrose's scouts brought him word of the single troop
and of the small numbers of the enemy's infantry.   He
ordered an attack, and his horsemen were moving
forward when suddenly a hundred dragoons charged
down on them, beating them back on the infantry, who
had not yet formed into line.   Then came the rest of

Strachan's cavalry and his musketeers. The Orcadians dropped their weapons and fled, to be cut down as they ran, or drowned in the water of the Kyle. The Danes fought manfully, as befitted the race they came of, but all their gallantry was in vain. The survivors were forced to surrender.

Montrose had his horse shot under him. He escaped from the field, however, and made his way to the glens. One night he sought shelter from the laird of Assynt, whose name of Macleod seemed to promise honour and loyalty. It was a misplaced trust. A price was on Montrose's head, and, false to every tradition of his clan, Assynt gave his guest into the hands of his foes. It is the solitary instance, in all the history of the Highlands, where a man was betrayed for gold. There is some satisfaction to us in the knowledge that the money seems never to have been paid.

On the 21st of May, 1650, on a gallows at the Mercat Cross of Edinburgh, James Graham laid down for his king the life he had so often ventured on the battlefield in that same cause.

NEWBURN (29th August, 1640).—When it became apparent that war between Charles I and his Scottish subjects was inevitable, the Scots proceeded to raise an army of 20,000 men, entrusting the command of it to Alexander Leslie. The king, having dissolved his English parliament which refused to help him in his struggle with Scotland, collected a considerable body of troops and marched towards the Border. With their vanguard led by Montrose, the Scots crossed the Tweed on the 20th of August, 1640. Nine days later they scattered the royal force which opposed them at Newburn on Tyne, and the following day they entered Newcastle. There they dictated to the king their terms, every one of which was ultimately granted.

PRESTON (17th August, 1648).—Scotland had no sympathy with the treatment of Charles I by his parlia-

mentarian enemies.   In April, 1648, an ultimatum was
sent to the English parliament, demanding, among other
things, the liberation of the king.   Believing in stronger
measures, the duke of Hamilton led into England an
army of 10,000 men.   In Lancashire he was joined by
several thousand English royalists, ill organised and badly
equipped.   With a somewhat smaller force, Cromwell
hurried north to meet the invaders, whom he defeated
with great loss at Preston on 17th August, and scattered
in further fighting on the two following days at Wigan
and Warrington.

Miracle on the Forth for Oliver Cromwell

DUNBAR.

(3rd September, 1650.)

THE Presbyterians of Lowland Scotland had the strongest objection to King Charles I as a religious dictator. Their faith was a matter solely for themselves and their own consciences, with which neither pope nor king might dare to interfere. To the house of Stewart, however, they were entirely loyal. There was no trace in them of the republicanism which formed so large a part of the policy of the English sectaries. Cromwell, the chief protagonist of that quack remedy for political ills, they hated like Lucifer, whose apostle, indeed, they believed him to be.

They esteemed him at what was probably more near to his real worth than have been the conceptions of certain historians, two Scotsmen among them, who have chosen to see in him a great man and a liberator, instead of a fanatical boor and one of the worst oppressors the isles of Britain have ever groaned under. In Scotland the Lord Protector was told to his face that he was a servant of sin, when Zachary Boyd preached to him in the Barony Kirk of Glasgow. In Scotland he missed, by a lucky change of route, being blown suddenly to the heavenly mansions he prated of, as he came into Glasgow by way of the Bishop's Castle, whose cellars were stored with gunpowder, ready for the match to be applied as he and his staff rode past. And it was in Scotland that he had his "crowning mercy"—from God or the devil as we may look at it.

The news of the murder of the king at Whitehall, murder in the trappings of justice, was received by the people of Scotland with horrified indignation. They

M   167

had done their best to protect his person, little though they liked his principles, having even, the year before, sent an army under the duke of Hamilton into England, where it had been cut up by Cromwell, and the duke made prisoner, shortly to be executed. Now that the king was dead, they hastened to shew their detestation of the action of the sectaries, and to fling defiance at Cromwell and his parliament, by proclaiming the younger Charles king of Great Britain, France and Ireland.

They were a strange people, though. They made this demonstration of loyalty to the crown; but when the greatest royalist among them came back from exile, they sent an army against him, and James Graham, Marquis of Montrose, was taken and hanged as any felon might have been.

On the 23rd of June, 1650, the young king landed at the mouth of the Spey. He had submerged his scruples, and signed both the National Covenant and the Solemn League; he would probably have signed anything at the time. Now he was in full favour with his loyal people, who installed him in Falkland Palace, and engaged relays of preachers to strengthen his faith in the pure doctrine of Presbyterianism. They were resolved to have a king, but this time they would have a hand in the shaping of him.

Cromwell was furiously angry, and possibly a little alarmed, when he learned of the turn of affairs in the north. He had imagined that the heads of all the Stewarts were on the neck of Charles I; yet here was one of them very much alive in Scotland. Strong and immediate action was urgently called for, so, with 16,000 men, he crossed the Border and marched on Edinburgh.

Meantime, the Scots had not been idle. They had collected an army for the protection of their king, and placed it under the command of David Leslie. In point of numbers, it was considerably stronger than Cromwell's force, but in military qualities it seems to have been sadly lacking, being led, according to a writer of the

period, "mainly by ministers' sons, clerks, and such other
sanctified creatures, who hardly ever saw or heard of any
sword but that of the Spirit." It was controlled by a
parliamentary committee, composed largely of ministers,
which did not scruple to dictate to Leslie and to over-ride
his experienced judgement whenever it saw fit.

On the 22nd of July, 1650, Cromwell had entered
Scotland, after assuring "his brethren in evil of a more
easy conquest of that kingdom than all the English
kings ever had." (Baillie.) Since none of them had
ever succeeded in such an object, he was promising less
than perhaps he imagined. Leslie was waiting for him,
in a strong position between Leith and Edinburgh, with
an army of 26,000 men.

The Scottish commander, who had fought Montrose
and finally beaten him, was an able leader, but on his
parliamentary committee, modelled apparently on the
lines of a kirk session, he had such a handicap as few
generals can ever have been hampered with. Their
first determination was that their armed forces should be
strong in the Word, whatever they might be in the field.
No back-slider should be in their ranks, no man however
good with sword and pike, who was not above suspicion
in the matter of the Covenant. A series of court-
martials were therefore established, and before the end
of August, with Cromwell and his formidable array close
at hand, some four thousand men were expelled from
the Scottish army for lack of godliness. As will readily
be understood, these were almost the whole of the real
soldiers in Leslie's command. The clerks and the
ministers' sons were left to him.

On 28th July Cromwell established his camp at Musselburgh. Somewhat to his surprise, he found the people
of Scotland as determinedly hostile to England and
Englishmen as ever their forebears had been. They
were so blindly stubborn that they refused to recognise
in him a protector, and saw only an invader as detestable
as any Plantagenet or Tudor.

He decided to make an appeal to their commonsense, and besought "God's elect in Scotland" to ally themselves with their fellow-elect across the Border. To the ministers, who, he realised, were his most bitter opponents, he addressed a special appeal. "I beseech you," he wrote "in the bowels of Christ, think it possible you may be mistaken." In particular, he urged them to read the twenty-eighth chapter of Isaiah, from the fifth to the fifteenth verse; but if he believed that Scottish ministers may ever be persuaded to admit that "they err in vision, they stumble in judgement," his experience of the race must have been a limited one. All his arguments and his texts fell unheeded on deaf ears, and he realised that if Scotland was to be won it could only be with the sword.

He decided, therefore, without more ado, to make an effort to capture Leith, and so secure a base for his shipping, through which much-needed supplies might reach his army. He quickly found that he was matched against a general who knew more about the strategy of war than he himself did. Leslie occupied a position which completely commanded both Leith and Edinburgh; and, although the Ironsides attacked him gallantly enough, they were driven off with considerable loss and pursued back to Musselburgh by Leslie's horse.

Now followed several weeks of manoeuvring, marching, and counter-marching. Cromwell was in serious straits. The harbour at Musselburgh was quite inadequate for his needs, and, unless he could secure a better base, he was threatened with famine. As it was, during a month he lost 5000 men, mainly from disease brought on by exposure and insufficient food.

Giving up all hope of taking Leith, he made several attempts on Queensferry, but each time he was outwitted by Leslie, whose superior military genius and more intimate local knowledge enabled him to seize the key positions which commanded every approach to the firth of Forth.

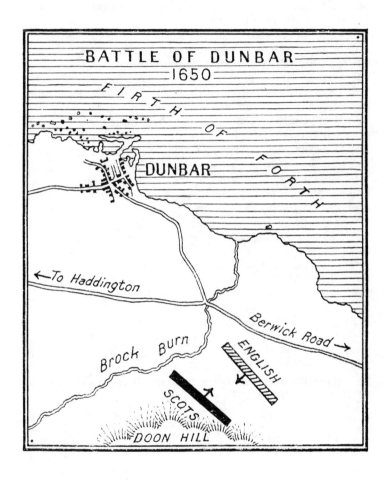

BATTLE OF DUNBAR
1650

Cromwell was forced to move southward, and still he was out-generaled. He fell back on Dunbar, which he reached on the 1st of September, and that same day Leslie's men occupied the Doon Hill, a commanding height to the south of the town. There was no shaking off the determined Scot, who next despatched a force to occupy the Pease Bridge, a narrow pass controlling the road to Berwick.

Cromwell was in a trap, which would not be easily got out of. His enemies blocked his way to the south. If he attempted to force a passage, he would have to fight with all the advantages against him, and could scarcely hope for success. To retreat by sea was impossible. The weather was stormy; he had not enough ships to accommodate all his men; and, apart from those difficulties, embarkation, with Leslie's troopers hovering around and ready to pounce at any favourable opportunity, would probably have cost him half his force. He said himself, in a letter, that escape would require "almost a miracle."

The situation could scarcely have been worse. Yet stout-hearted Oliver did not despair. "We have much hope in the Lord," he wrote, "of Whose mercy we have had large experience." He was to be justified in his confidence. The miracle happened.

On the evening of the 2nd of September, the English were astounded to see the Scots coming down from their hill. All night through, columns of them filed down on to the plain, and by morning they had given up the whole of their advantage. To Cromwell it must have seemed that Leslie had gone mad.

The ministers had been at work again, teaching their general his business. In vain he pointed out that he had manoeuvred the English force into a position from which their escape was practically impossible, and that in time they would be compelled by famine to surrender. There was no need for the Scots to risk the uncertain outcome of a battle. But the committee of amateur tacticians were impatient. The Lord had been good to them. Victory was within their reach. Let them snatch it without further delay.

Some of the preachers put a sudden end to the argument by marshalling their flocks and leading them down the hillside. Leslie could do nothing else than follow.

When Cromwell saw the new position taken up by the Scots, well might he exclaim, as he is said to have done, "the Lord hath delivered them into my hands." They had the Brock Burn, within its deep banks, on their left; behind them was the steep slope of the hill: if they failed to achieve a speedy success they would find it impossible either to retire or to execute a change of front. They would be completely hemmed in when once he had taken up the position he contemplated.

Before daybreak, on 3rd September, the English began to move south from Dunbar. With a body of horse and two regiments of foot, they made good the passage of the burn, near the spot where it is crossed by the Berwick road. The Scottish pickets were driven back, and the entire English force passed safely over the stream, to take up a line facing the Scots and closing the box in which those unfortunates had put themselves.

The attack began as soon as the two armies were opposite each other. The onset was by the English. Lambert's brigade and Monk's made the first advance. They were received with the greatest resolution, and forced to retire with considerable loss. Then Cromwell himself led forward three regiments of foot and one of horse. They, too, were stoutly met by the men to whom Leslie had entrusted his first line. But Cromwell's troops were fresh. The others had already fought Monk and Lambert. The Ironsides forced their way on, till they had only the clerks and ministers' sons to deal with. Those gentlemen promptly fled, throwing the whole army into confusion. The battle was over. Two regiments "fought it out manfully, and were all killed as they stood." Of the rest, many surrendered

immediately; the remainder of the "sanctified creatures"
threw away their weapons and ran, with the English
dragoons hard on their heels, cutting them down in
swathes.

At Dunbar the Scots had three thousand killed, and
lost some ten thousand prisoners. The English losses
must have been trifling, as it was in their flight that
most of the Scots were slain.

Had Leslie been allowed to retain his ungodly veterans,
there would probably have been a different ending to the
battle, and a different course to the subsequent history
of Britain. He himself declared, in a letter to Argyll,
"I take God to witness we might have as easily beaten
them as we did James Graham at Philiphaugh, if the
officers had stayed by their troops and regiments."

As it was, Cromwell was to trample on liberty for
several years more. He died on the 3rd of September,
1658. It might have been eight years earlier to the day,
if David Leslie had had a free hand and his own men at
Dunbar.

CROMWELL

Race to London for Keys to the Kingdom!

WORCESTER.

(3rd September, 1651.)

FULLY half of the Scottish army was lost at Dunbar. With what was left to him, Leslie managed to make his escape and retired into the fortresses of the north, there to attempt to recruit his forces.

Edinburgh and Leith had fallen into the hands of Cromwell immediately after the battle. Glasgow and other southern towns he quickly occupied in their turn, until soon he was master of the whole of the country south of the Forth and the Clyde.

In the Highlands, however, there was a considerable force of royalists, under the command of Major Middleton, eager to take the field on a suitable opportunity. In the north, also, the king had a body of adherents in the ever loyal district of Aberdeen. These troops were gradually organised, and brought into touch with each other and with Leslie.

On the 1st of January, 1651, Charles was solemnly crowned at Scone as king of Great Britain and Ireland. His capitals were in the hands of his enemies, so he held his little court, and listened to his sermons, first at Dunfermline and later at Perth. There a meeting of parliament was held in May, and it was resolved to raise another army, of which Leslie was to be the commander and Middleton his Master of Horse. Very wisely, for once, it was decided that no qualifications of piety would be required of the recruits; so the services of the Highlanders and the Aberdeen men were made available, and, what was even more important, the general could get back his old officers who had been drummed out before Dunbar.

175

When he had gathered a sufficient force around him, Leslie established himself on the high ground, known as the Torwood, between Stirling and Falkirk, a place of strength much favoured by both Wallace and Bruce. There he encamped his army, and made a fortification around it, resisting all the attempts of Cromwell to entice him out of it before he was ready to come.

The English general became exasperated as he saw this opposition to his schemes rapidly growing. Deciding that action must quickly be taken, he collected his troops, which were scattered over the south country, crossed the Forth at Queensferry, drove off a royalist party which attempted to stop him at Inverkeithing, and, marching rapidly northward, occupied Perth.

Now, thought Leslie, had come his opportunity. He was actually between the English troops and their own country, with an open road before him. While they were entangled among the hills of the north, where they could do little harm, he would push south with all speed and invade England.

He had with him some 12,000 men, perhaps the greater part of them Highlanders. In England, particularly in Lancashire and Cheshire, where popular sympathy was very largely royalist, he hoped to pick up many recruits in passing.

Cromwell, who may have anticipated Leslie's move, at once took steps to counter it. Leaving Monk in charge of affairs in Scotland, he himself, with the bulk of his troops, set off for the south. Leslie, with whom was the young king, had three days start.

It was necessary for the Scots to take the western route, by Carlisle and Lancaster, as the easier road by Berwick and the east coast was held by detachments of Cromwell's men. The only chance of success lay in rapidity of movement. If London was reached, with the three days start still maintained, it was by no means unreasonable to hope that Charles's friends in England would take fresh heart, and rally to his standard in sufficient numbers to win back his throne for him. There was no time to be lost, however.

It was a race for London. Cromwell fully realised his danger, and pressed with all speed down the east road, while Leslie hurried down the west.

Leslie had left Stirling on the 31st of July. On the 7th of August, he reached Penrith, having thus covered more than 140 miles in seven days, good marching on the roads of the time. At Penrith, Charles was proclaimed as king of England, and at the market cross of Lancaster the proclamation was repeated on the 12th. Two days later the army was within a few hours march of Warrington.

In Lancashire Leslie met with the disappointment which Scottish royalists and Jacobites have always been fated to receive there. As later, in 1715 and 1745, the legitimists of the north of England had apparently more heart for drinking loyal toasts behind shuttered windows than for risking their lives and their property in an armed rising on behalf of their principles.

Warrington and the bridge over the Mersey were found to be held by a flying detachment of Cromwell's troops, which, with remarkable speed, had pushed so far ahead of the main body as to have now managed actually to be in front of the Scots. Their numbers were few, however, and, although they put up a good fight, the town was carried by mid-day and the bridge in the afternoon.

Refusing to be tempted to turn aside from his route in order to pursue the retreating Roundheads, Leslie pressed steadily on, still covering almost twenty miles a day, and, six days after leaving Warrington, entered Worcester. Here it was decided that a brief halt was imperative, to rest the men and horses, and repair the wastage of equipment inevitable on so long a march.

Four days after the Scots reached Worcester, Cromwell entered Evesham, and the two forces were practically in touch.

Leslie had chosen well in making Worcester his first halting place. It was a walled city of considerable strength, and further protected by the deep and rapid Severn which must be crossed by Cromwell before he could launch an attack.

On the 2nd September the pursuers were discovered making a bridge of boats a little way below the town. Leslie sent some troops to interfere with this manoeuvre but they were too few for the purpose and were driven off. Soon the bridge was completed, and Cromwell's army passed over the river, to join hands with a strong force, under Fleetwood, which had come from the south.

Next day, the anniversary of Dunbar, Worcester, was attacked. The Scots were outnumbered by about three to one; but they offered a gallant resistance, defending themselves in the castle and at the Sudbury Gate. For three hours the castle held out; then it was taken by assault. At the Sudbury Gate the Scots clung to their ground for two hours more, until they were overwhelmed by the vastly superior force against them.

Leslie was captured. His army was annihilated. The king, with a few followers, managed to elude his conqueror, but escape was impossible for any considerable remnant of the defeated troops. Those who were not slain were made prisoners, to be sent to slavery in the West Indies.

Worcester was the last battle of the Civil War. It gave Cromwell the mastery of the whole island of Britain from the Channel to the Pentland Firth. He had fulfilled his boast, and done what no English king could do, reduced Scotland to the bondage under which she was to suffer for ten years. As a country she virtually did not exist from that day until the Restoration.

DALNASPIDAL (July, 1654).—After the battle of Worcester the greater part of Scotland submitted to its apparently inevitable fate. In the Highlands, however, a little army of royalists continued in the field, awaiting a

favourable opportunity to strike another blow for the
king. At Dalnaspidal, at the head of Loch Garry, they
came into contact with a portion of Cromwell's army of
occupation, and, in a confused engagement in a narrow
pass, the royalists were defeated. This was the last attempt in Scotland to break the power of the "Protector."

RULLION GREEN (28th November, 1666).—The restoration of the Stewarts brought to Scotland none of the
happiness that had been eagerly looked for. With
almost incredible ingratitude towards the country
which had shed so much of its best blood in his cause,
Charles II, immediately he was on the throne, set
himself to trample on the civil and religious liberties of
the Scots, ignoring every promise which he had made
to them when in them lay his only hope. Rebellion
became inevitable. It began in Dumfries, and spread
rapidly to Ayrshire and Lanarkshire. In November,
1666, a force of insurgents, 3000 strong, began a march
to Edinburgh, pursued by government troops under
Sir Thomas Dalziel. Poorly armed and with no organi-
sation, the rebels suffered from so many desertions that
when they reached Colinton their number had been
reduced to less than a thousand. Discovering that no
support was to be looked for in the capital, they turned
about, taking the road to the west over the Pentland
hills. At Rullion Green they were attacked by Dalziel's
dragoons. The rebels stood their ground well; but,
though fighting stubbornly, they had to give way before
the more experienced and better equipped troops who
opposed them. The Pentland Rising, as it was called,
was followed by wholesale executions of men suspected
of disaffection to the government. It was then that
the Lord Advocate of the day earned, perhaps undeser-
vedly, his title of "Bluidy Mackenzie."

Fiasco of the 'pitchfork' army

DRUMCLOG AND BOTHWELL BRIDGE

(1st *June*, 1679; 22nd *June*, 1679.)

THE campaign, if such it may be called, of Drumclog and Bothwell Bridge would scarcely deserve memory but for the romantic fables which have been woven around it by those who, through lack of information or by deliberate ignoring of facts, have chosen to regard the Covenanters of that period as persecuted saints suffering for righteousness sake. Such a description might well enough be applied to the ministers who, after the return of the bishops on the restoration of Charles II, chose to leave their manses and their parishes and take to the hills and moors rather than be false to their principles. The great body of Covenanters, however, both before and after that time, were men who, inspired more by political than religious motives, took up arms against the king's government and must be held to have accepted all the consequences which such an act entailed.

An armed rising had been threatening for several years. The unrest was brought to a head by the murder on Magus Moor.

James Sharp was the most detested prelate in Scotland. There was good reason why he should be. Sent to London to uphold the cause of presbyterianism, he had come back the anointed archbishop of St. Andrews and the object of the hatred of every faithful Covenanter in the land. On the 3rd of May, 1679, while driving across Magus Moor, his coach was stopped by a party of his enemies, and, on his knees, praying for his life, he was stabbed in a hundred places by their swords. The two principal men among the assassins were Hackston of

180

Rathillet, whose hand had no actual part in the killing, and John Balfour of Kinloch, commonly called Burley.

Their deed done, the murderers posted to the west, where they knew they would find friends in plenty to uphold them. They were not disappointed. The Covenanters of Clydesdale were in a mood for insurrection, and welcomed the opportunity to carry on the work begun at St. Andrews. The 29th of May was approaching, the day appointed by government for rejoicing on the anniversary of the king's restoration, and they determined to celebrate it in their own way. They would burn all the acts of parliament passed since the king's return to the throne.

For this demonstration of their faith they would have preferred Glasgow to be the scene, but that city was strongly held by royal troops and the nearest they dared come to it was to the little burgh of Rutherglen. At the cross of that town, on the king's own bonfire, they duly consigned his obnoxious enactments to the flames. This picturesque ceremony had the hoped for effect. The malcontents from the surrounding country came hurrying in, and assembled in the neighbourhood of Strathaven.

A cavalry officer, John Graham of Claverhouse, with two troops, about 180 men in all, went out from Glasgow to deal with them. He found them drawn up in order of battle at the farm of Drumclog, near Loudon Hill, on the morning of Sunday, the 1st of June. They had chosen their position skilfully. In front of them was a deep ditch and all around were bogs. Their number has been variously estimated. The nearest we can come to it is perhaps from the report of Claverhouse, who states that they had four battalions of foot and three squadrons of horse, perhaps a thousand men all told. From their easy victory we may assume that that estimate is probably correct.

Across the bog the two forces fired at each other for some time, with as little effect as the musketry of that period usually produced. Claverhouse, we may be sure from what we know of him, would gladly have come to closer quarters, but he had no-one to guide his men through the morass. His enemies solved the difficulty for him. Led by William Cleland, a young man who was later to become a famous soldier as the first colonel of the Cameronians, a large party of them made their way round the ditch and threw themselves on the dragoons.

So boldly and with such determination was the attack made that it met with instant success. The dragoons were thrown into disorder, and seem to have made little effort to defend themselves. Thirty-six of them were killed, seven were made prisoners, and the rest put spurs to their horses and galloped off to Strathaven, their commander with them, his horse's belly ripped open by a pitchfork.

Five of the prisoners were released by their captors, a fact which very much grieved the Covenanting leader, Robert Hamilton, when he heard of it. He got some satisfaction for his disappointment by shooting one of the remaining two with his own hand. This was not the only act of savagery perpetrated by the godly victors that Sabbath morning. Among the king's officers who had been killed was a cornet named Graham, a relative of Claverhouse. His body was mistaken for that of his leader, so his eyes were gouged out, his tongue was torn from his mouth, and his nose and ears were cut off, an example of malevolent hatred fortunately without parallel in Scottish history.

The dragoons retired to Glasgow, where Claverhouse put up defences around the Mercat Cross, barricades and breastworks across the streets, in anticipation of an attempt by the Covenanters to follow up their victory. They made it the next morning, but it was a faint-hearted and ill-organised attack which was easily beaten off.

The success at Drumclog fired the spirit of all the Covenanters of the west. They came pouring into

Lanarkshire, from Renfrewshire, Ayrshire and all the country round about, until they numbered close on 6000 men, armed with whatever weapons they could lay their hands on, muskets, pikes, swords, pitchforks and scythe blades.   For leader they chose Robert Hamilton again.   He was a man of family, brother to the laird of Preston, but he was completely devoid both of military experience and the genius for command.   He was chosen in preference to men like Hackston, who had served with the Prince of Orange, solely on account of his fanatical enthusiasm.   His one thought was to kill the "Amalekites," and all his talk was of it; he seemed incapable of realising that they might take a hand in the game.

The government took a serious view of the rising.   To make certain of stamping it out with all possible speed, an army of 15,000 men was allotted to the task.   In command was put the ill-fated natural son of the king, the duke of Monmouth, who had become duke of Buccleuch on marrying the heiress of that house.

On the morning of the 22nd, the two forces faced each other across the Clyde at the bridge of Bothwell, the insurgents on the south bank, the king's men on the north.   The Covenanting army was a mere rabble, with no attempt at military formation such as men like Hackston and Cleland would have insisted on.   Those, and others like them, were allowed no authority by the ministers, who exhorted their flocks to slay and were content to trust the Lord to arrange how it was to be done.   Hamilton himself, the nominal commander-in-chief, had other business on hand than seeing to his line of battle.   He was superintending the erection of a huge gibbet, on which he meant to hang his prisoners, with several cart-loads of rope which he had brought along for the purpose.

It cannot be called a battle, the affair at Bothwell. The only man on the Covenant side who made any show of generalship was Hackston of Rathillet.   He

N

had no instructions, but he collected a handful of reliable men, and with them he held the south end of the bridge while his ammunition lasted. Then he was compelled to fall back, and Monmouth's troops marched quietly across. Their passage was undisputed, and they met with but the slightest opposition as they surrounded their opponents.

Twelve hundred Covenanters were taken prisoners, and were tried in Edinburgh. Two were executed there, and five others were hanged on Magus Moor in expiation of the murder although none of them had had any hand in it. Of the remainder, a large number were released on parole; the others were deported.

Deadly musket fire failed to stop clans' determined charge

KILLIECRANKIE.

(27th July, 1689.)

A STRANGE position, in the memory of the Scots, is that occupied by John Graham of Claverhouse, Viscount Dundee. People will be heard referring almost in a single breath to Bloody Clavers and Bonnie Dundee, the ruthless persecutor and the national hero, without quite realising, apparently, that these two are but one individual.

For centuries Covenanting sentimentalism painted Dundee as a savage brute, utterly devoid of human feeling, a devil incarnate. It is only within very recent years that the slanders on his name have been refuted and his true nature understood. He was a soldier, and as such he carried out faithfully his duty against the rebels, for it must not be forgottten that rebels the Covenanters were, engaged in armed defiance of the Government, not poor defenceless creatures whose only wish was to be allowed to conduct their religious rites in peace.

It is interesting to consider for a moment the record for humanity of Claverhouse and of the men he is accused of having persecuted. It has been constantly asserted that with his own hands Claverhouse despatched innocent men, women and children, for no other fault than their faith, but the only example ever adduced is that of John Brown of Priestfield, the famous "Christian Carrier." John Brown, it is known, certainly received summary justice, but it was from a firing squad, after a considerable store of arms and treasonable papers had been found in his house, and he had firmly refused to promise not to rise in arms against the king. Not a single instance can be shewn of Claverhouse ordering the death

185

of a woman or child; but it is established beyond dispute that, after Philiphaugh, three hundred Highland and Irish women, with their children, were butchered in cold blood by the soldiers of the Covenant on the express command of their ministers. Even the stern Leslie was sickened by the spectacle, and appealed to the minister of Newmilns, "Mr. John, have you not once gotten your fill of blood?"

If it comes to weighing in the balance of humanity and virtue John Graham against the "persecuted saints," the scales come heavily down on the side of Claverhouse. Every action of his life was consistent with the honour of a soldier, one of the best criterions by which a man may be judged. We must give credit to the Covenanters for their readiness to endure suffering and death without flinching, but, when they had power in their hands, even their most fervent apologist cannot deny that they were guilty of barbarities such as never stained the name of royalist.

Graham of Claverhouse, "Dark John of the Battles," as his Highlanders called him, came of a family that had ever been loyal adherents of the Stewarts. They were cadets of the house of Montrose. He himself served Charles II and James VII in many positions of trust, and was rewarded by the grant, among other distinctions, of a peerage, as Viscount Dundee. When he was but a little over forty, he had risen from the comparative obscurity of an Angus laird to be one of the foremost men in the kingdom. He was not long to enjoy his honours, however.

On the 4th of April, 1689, the Scottish parliament made the momentous declaration which was to cost Scotland rivers of blood. "The Estates of the kingdom of Scotland find and declare that King James the Seventh, being a profest Papist, did assume the regal power and acted as king without taking the oath required by law, and hath by the advice of evil and wicked councillors invaded the fundamental constitution of this kingdom, and

altered it from a legal limited monarchy to an arbitrary
despotic power, and hath exercised the same to the
subversion of the Protestant religion and the violation of
the laws and liberties of the nation, inverting all the
ends of government, whereby he hath forefaulted the
right to the crown, and the throne is become vacant."

A fortnight before this resolution of the Estates was
passed, Dundee had strode indignantly out of the Convention, put himself at the head of a band of his troopers,
given a last message to the duke of Gordon, who with a
tiny garrison was gallantly holding Edinburgh Castle for
King James, and ridden off to his castle of Dudhope. A
message was sent after him, summoning him to return
at once to Edinburgh and take his seat in the Convention.
He excused himself, and, knowing that the now ruling
party would be certain to attempt his arrest, for they
would not dare to leave so formidable an enemy at
liberty and openly hostile, he retired into the Highlands,
where, amid the Jacobite clans, he knew that he would
be safe. On the 30th of March he was proclaimed a
traitor at the Cross of Edinburgh, a fact which is likely
to have troubled him little.

Most of the Highland clans were strongly for James.
Dundee's first object was to confirm them in their loyalty,
and persuade them to raise from among their hardy
fighting men an army which would bring back the king
and set him on his throne again. For that purpose,
with a troop of his old regiment behind him, he made a
tour of a great part of the north.

First he went to Glen Ogilvy, where he remained for
three days at his wife's jointure-house, having conferences
with various chiefs and lairds. Then he rode north,
passing over Cairn-o'-Mount, to Kincardine O'Neil. By
the 21st of April he was at Keith rallying the loyal men
of Banffshire. From there he went to Elgin, where Provost
Stewart and the bailies gave him a welcome which afterwards the Convention made them pay for. At Forres
he halted. It was a suitable place for meetings with the

chiefs of the north-western clans, the majority of whom, particularly Cameron of Lochiel, had given indications of readiness to take the field for the king.

In the Lowlands, too, there were Jacobite murmurings, inspired probably not so much by love of James as of Claverhouse. Two officers of his old regiment of dragoons made their way secretly to Dudhope, and asked Lady Dundee to send word to her husband that his troopers were ready to join him to a man whenever he would send for them.

Dundee received the welcome news, and resolved to move south to meet the regiment and put himself at its head so soon as possible. At Cairn-o'-Mount, however, there was caught a messenger from the Master of Forbes to General Mackay, the commander of the Government forces, and it was learned that Mackay, who was close at hand with three regiments of foot and one of horse, had made elaborate plans to surround the little party of rebels. Dundee turned again and made for Castle Gordon where he was joined by the earl of Dunfermline and about fifty other gentlemen.

Meanwhile the clans were rapidly rising; not without certain of the troubles almost inseparable from such an assembly. Old feuds were remembered and revived, and it required at times all the diplomatic skill of Dundee to preserve the peace. More than diplomacy sometimes, in fact, as when MacDonald of Keppoch, finding himself at the head of eight hundred men, decided to pay off an old score on the burgh of Inverness, and, laying siege to the town, enforced a payment of four thousand merks which he claimed to be owing to him. Dundee could keep the goodwill of both parties only by allowing the chief to keep the cash, and giving the town a receipt for it in name of the king.

There were not many chiefs like Keppoch, the "Colonel of the Cows." The majority were men of high honour, honestly inspired by sentiments of loyalty to the house of Stewart; and they promised support to Dundee in such numbers that soon he was assured of the adherence of almost every notable clan, unless such as the Campbells, the Grants, and the Forbeses. On the 7th of May, from the remote farmhouse of Presmukerach, near Dalwhinnie, he issued, in the king's name, an order to all loyal men then in arms to meet him in Lochaber on the 18th of that month.

The time until the rendezvous he occupied in an endeavour to obtain more recruits and enlist further sympathy for his cause. On the 10th of May he was at Dunkeld, having eluded the pursuing Mackay. There he came on an agent who was collecting taxes in the name of the Government, so he quietly annexed the money and the horses and arms of the military escort. At Perth he captured two local lairds and some officers who were engaged there in raising a troop of militia for Mackay. Then, by way of Scone, Cupar-Angus and Meigle, he approached Dundee, where his old regiment was awaiting him. Captain Livingstone, one of his officers still with the regiment, had his plans ready. He asked leave to make a sortie, to drive off the rebels, with his dragoons and a party of three hundred Jacobite townsmen whom he had got together. He was forbidden, however, and Dundee had to go off again without his hoped for reinforcement of trained men.

By the 18th of May, Dundee was in Lochaber, and within a week his Highland army had assembled. Sir Ewen Cameron of Lochiel brought one thousand men, the MacDonald chiefs led a thousand more, and MacLean of Duart the same. The Stewarts of Appin were there, the MacNeills of Barra, the Macleods of Skye and Raasay, the Frasers, the Macnaughtons, the Macallisters, the Maclachlans and the Lamonts. Perhaps four thousand men in all had answered the summons. Besides these, there was Dundee's small body of cavalry, some eighty in all, composed of a troop of his old dragoons and a number of private gentlemen.

Now came a kind of military "general post." Mackay

was at Alvie, and Dundee set off to look for him there,
taking, in passing, the castle of Ruthven; while Keppoch,
to his commander's intense annoyance, paid off an old
score on the Macintoshes by burning their castle of
Dunachton.

At Alvie, Mackay's camp was found to be deserted,
and his troops flown. They were not long gone, so the
Highlanders pressed on at their heels, sometimes coming
within musket-shot of the rearguard. This lasted
for four days, until the more open country at Strathbogie
was approached. Mackay's very great superiority in
cavalry would have given him a tremendous advantage
here, so Dundee called a halt, although Mackay continued
to push on.

Dundee's intelligence service was excellent, as was
only to be expected with so many of his old friends
and secret sympathisers in the enemy's camp. He
learned that his opponent had been reinforced by two
fresh regiments; also that his old troopers were now
so closely surrounded by English dragoons that it was
impossible in the meantime for them to desert to him,
that, in fact, they might even be compelled to fight
against him if there were an immediate engagement.
He was advised, therefore, to retire for a little.

He took the advice, and ordered a retiral towards
Badenoch. Mackay, encouraged by his increased strength,
pressed after him. On the 9th of June there was the
first clash of arms. An advance detachment of Mackay's
dragoons came up with a party of Macleans, three
hundred strong, who were hurrying to join Dundee. In
a brief but bloody engagement, the dragoons were
routed, leaving a considerable quantity of valuable
spoil in the hands of the Highlanders.

In a campaign in which there was little actual fighting,
a Highland army was a difficult thing to hold together,
especially when the majority of the men were at no
great distance from their own territory. Claverhouse
found that his clansmen, who had acquired a fair amount

of loot from their enemies in the Grant and Macintosh country, were now becoming impatient to get away with their plunder. So he passed into Lochaber, and allowed all who so wished to go home. Furlough it might be called, for they were under promise to return whenever they were summoned. It was a wise move not to attempt to impose too rigid a discipline on the untamed Highlanders. They would have gone off in any case, whenever they felt inclined, and might not have come too readily back again. As it was, their response to his next call was prompt and enthusiastic.

From the middle of June till the middle of July, Dundee lay quietly in Lochaber. An offer of terms was made to him through his brother-in-law, Lord Strathnever; but he refused it indignantly. Then, realising that he was completely irreconcilable to them, the Government declared him an outlaw and put on his head a price of £20,000. They might have saved themselves their pains. No money could have secured his betrayal by the loyal Celts, who would cut an enemy's throat as readily as a sheep's, but would not sell a friend for all the gold in England.

For a month the two forces kept apart, until the affair of Blair Castle brought them together again. That strong fortress, belonging to the marquis of Atholl, occupied one of the most important strategic positions in Scotland, commanding the passes into the valleys of the Dee and the Spey. The marquis was in London, having left his son, Lord John Murray, in charge at Blair. To Murray Dundee wrote several letters urging that the castle should be held for King James. Murray, who seems to have been in touch with Mackay, made no reply. Dundee therefore instructed the factor of the estate, Stewart of Ballochin, a trusty Jacobite, to use his influence with the clansmen, which he did to such good purpose that they let it be plainly known to Murray that no Englishman or Dutchman would set a foot in their stronghold.

It now became a race for the castle between Mackay and Dundee.   The latter had summoned his Highlanders again, and bidden them be at Blair by the 26th of July, on which date he himself arrived there with his small band of horsemen.   On the same day Mackay arrived at Dunkeld, with "six battalions of foot, four troops of horse and as many dragoons," perhaps four thousand men in all.

A considerable part of Dundee's force had not yet arrived, so a council of war was held at Blair, to decide whether it would be wise to engage an enemy who outnumbered the Highlanders by at least three to two, or if it would not be more prudent to retire until all the clans were assembled.   The majority seemed to favour the latter policy; but, when the question was put to Lochiel, he said without a word of hesitation, "Let us fight," urging as his reason the obvious high spirits of the men.   Dundee was so emphatically of the same opinion that immediate action was decided on.   Then Lochiel arose again, and said he had one request to make, a stipulation in which was involved perhaps the whole chance of success of the king's cause.

However the day might go with them, their leader must take no part in the fight.   Too much depended on the life of Dundee for him to risk it like a common soldier's.   Let them win or lose, he must live to follow up the victory, or retrieve their fortunes after the defeat.

This was wise counsel, but difficult for a man of Dundee's temperament to accept.   What, he said, would his men think of him.   They would doubt his courage.   Let him give but one "shear-darg" (day's harvesting) to the king, and he promised that never again would he hazard his life during the campaign. With that they had perforce to be content.

Early in the morning of the 27th of July, Mackay marched out of Dunkeld, and by ten o'clock had reached the southern end of the Pass of Killiecrankie, a narrow

defile between steep and thickly wooded hills, with the
Garry, swift and deep, racing along the bottom of it.
The passage, two miles in length, was wide enough to
allow the troops to march through, but that was all.
With the mountains crushing in on each side of them,
they would be held firmly to the path.   There was not a
yard of ground on which to manoeuvre in the event of a
surprise by the enemy.

For two hours the troops halted at the beginning of
the pass.   Then they began to creep cautiously forward,
every moment expecting an attack by the Highlanders,
who, it was felt sure, must be lurking on the hillside.
But Dundee had no thought of an ambush and an indecisive action in the pass.   What he looked for was a
pitched battle in which he might strike a real blow for
the king.   To the surprise and relief of Mackay and
every man under him, the dangerous pass was traversed
without a hint of the presence of their foes.

Immediately the open ground at its further end was
reached, the army was drawn up for battle, facing towards
Blair, from which direction the attack was to be expected.
In the centre were the horse, rather an unusual arrangement.   On their left were posted the battalions of Balfour,
Ramsay, and Kenmore; on the right those of Leven,
Mackay himself, and Hastings.   Behind the horse were
some guns, small portable affairs of hooped leather from
which not much useful service could be looked for.

Presently the Highlanders were seen coming down the
valley, and the long line of horse and foot prepared to
meet them.   But no sooner had Mackay given his orders
to this purpose than he discovered that the oncomers
were only a small party sent to fix his attention, while
Dundee's main body was getting into position on the
hillside on the right flank.   A sudden change of direction
was necessary.   The line was swung round to the right,
and found itself in a most undesirable position.   Close
behind was the rushing Garry and the steep ridge beyond
it; in front was a rising hill.   To advance would be

difficult; in the event of defeat, to retire would be almost impossible. The only hope lay in speedy victory.

Dundee drew up his men in battalions also, with one facing each party of Mackay's troops. On the right were the Macleans; next to them an Irish contingent under Colonel Pearson; then Clanranald's men, Glengarry's, Lochiel's and Sir Donald Macdonald's. In the centre, confronting the two troops of horse, was his small body of cavalry, not more then forty sabres in all.

For some hours the two forces stood immobile, confronting each other. Mackay would not attack up the hillside, and Dundee refused to move while the strong sun was in the faces of his men. Only the leather guns indulged in an intermittent and perfectly harmless bombardment. It was eight o'clock in the evening when Dundee gave the word for his men to advance. Then the plaids were cast aside, and the Highlanders rushed down the slope towards their enemies, yelling the slogans of their clans. They were met by a deadly musket fire, which cut into their ranks but could not stop their determined charge. On they came, holding their fire, as they had been bidden, until they could be certain of doing most damage with it. They were no more than a few yards from the foremost rank of the enemy, when they discharged their muskets in one thunderous volley. Then, throwing their firearms away, they set on with their claymores, hewing and slashing like men possessed.

"Nothing was heard for some few moments," says Lochiel in his "Memoirs," "but the sullen and hollow clashes of the broadswords, with the dismal groans and cries of dying and wounded men."

Dundee had put himself in the first line of his horsemen. That little band, on their lean and wearied mounts, charged straight at the troops of regular cavalry, who did not wait to receive them, but wheeled about and fled for the pass.

One by one, Mackay's battalions were broken and

scattered. Only Leven's regiment (now the King's Own Scottish Borderers) stood to its ground, in spite of its terrible losses, and, managing to cross the river, made an orderly retreat. In killed and prisoners, the Government forces lost two thousand men. The Highlanders had nine hundred killed. And among them there was the one they could least afford to lose.

Seeing that the left of his attack was not so successful as the rest of the line, Dundee was riding forward to urge the men there on, when a musket bullet struck him in the side, and brought him from the saddle. One of his officers hurried to his aid; but his wound was a mortal one. In a few minutes he died, with the shouts of his victorious Highlanders for requiem. It was the death that before all others it is certain he would have chosen.

Wrapped in two tartan plaids, he was buried that night in the little church of Blair.

What Lochiel had feared was soon realised. With their commander gone, the Highlanders were not able to follow up their victory. Within a few days of the battle their numbers had increased to upwards of five thousand, a formidable array. But there was no one now to lead them. In August they were beaten off from Dunkeld by an army of west country Cameronians; and, after some desultory fighting during the winter, they were finally defeated in the following spring at the Haughs of Cromdale.

The cause of the Stewarts was lost for the time being. Perhaps it was at Killiecrankie that it was lost for ever, when John Graham of Claverhouse died.

DUNKELD (21st August, 1689).—Among the troops raised by the government to oppose Dundee and his Highlanders was a regiment of west-country Covenanters belonging to the sect of Cameronians. They were commanded by a young man who had fought at Drumclog and Bothwell Bridge, William Cleland. After Killiecrankie this regiment took up its position in Dunkeld, in the midst of hostile country, and refused to accept all advice, and even definite instructions, to abandon its dangerous quarters. There it was attacked by the Highland army under Colonel Cannon, Dundee's successor. Cannon had five thousand men, Cleland only twelve hundred; but the Cameronians were made of sterner stuff than their fellows who had turned tail at Killie-crankie. For many hours they withstood the full force of the Highland onslaught, fighting with reckless courage in the narrow streets, whose houses, fired by Cleland's men as they fell into the hands of their enemies, were by nightfall ablaze from one end of the little town to the other. In the cathedral and a neighbouring mansion the defenders finally established themselves, and there they held their ground, cutting bullets from the lead in the roofs of their strongholds, until the Highlanders, abandoning all hope of success, made off to the hills. Cleland was killed in the hour of victory. Such was the first fight of the 26th Foot, the Cameronians (Scottish Rifles.)

CROMDALE (1st May, 1690).—Throughout the winter of 1689-90, the Highland army, gradually diminishing in numbers, roamed about the north of Scotland. No serious attempt was made to bring it to battle until the late spring, when a column was despatched from Inverness under Colonel Livingstone, the commander of the garrison there. The Highlanders, encamped at Cromdale, about three miles north of Grantown, were surprised by a night attack. Before they had time to rally, about three hundred of them had been slain by Livingstone's troopers, and a hundred taken prisoner. The others escaped to the hills; but they were broken as an effective force and soon afterwards dispersed.

The Fiery Cross is sent through Highland Glens

SHERIFFMUIR.

(13th November, 1715.)

To understand the steadfast attachment of so large a part both of the Highlands and Lowlands of Scotland to the house of Stewart, it is necessary to realise all that lay behind it.   In 1715 and 1745, there were still Jacobites who, like Dundee's men, were inspired only by single-minded devotion to the legitimate royal house.   But they were probably a small minority.   A far greater number were prompted by the fact that in the restoration of the Stewarts they saw a way towards the dissolution of the Union between Scotland and England.

The Union had been brought about in face of the opposition of practically the whole of the Scottish people.   When it was mooted, protests poured in on the Scottish parliament from every part of the country. Glasgow and Edinburgh were in open insurrection; the Jacobite north and the Cameronian west, agreeing for the first time in history, were preparing to rise together in armed rebellion.   If only a leader of sufficient determination had been forthcoming, the people of Scotland would never have accepted the hateful measure.   But the hour did not bring forth the man.

On 25th March, 1707, "amid riot and uproar and with howls of execration sounding in their ears, the Estates of Scotland met for the last time."   (R. S. Rait.) Then Scotland ceased to be a separate kingdom.

Bitterly as the mass of the Scottish people were opposed to union with England, once the deed was done they were soon to be roused to greater anger still.   It became immediately apparent that the assembly at Westminster was determined to legislate with no thought of any interests save those of England.   As Hume Brown

197

describes it, "Every interest of Scotland was regarded and treated purely and simply with reference to the exigencies of political parties in England." The very terms of the Treaty of Union were shamelessly disregarded. Principal Rait gives instances in his "Making of Scotland."

"The Act of Union had provided that no court sitting in Westminster Hall should receive appeals from the Court of Session. In 1709, the House of Lords revised a decision of the Court of Session in a case in which the Presbytery of Edinburgh had prosecuted an Episcopal clergyman for reading the Anglican liturgy. In 1710, a Toleration Act was passed to protect Scottish Episcopalians, while English Presbyterians were almost simultaneously subjected to fresh disabilities. In 1712, by a gross breach of the agreement made at the Union, lay patronage was restored in the church of Scotland. New taxation pressed heavily on the Scots, who found that their trade had rather diminished than increased."

The new taxation was of the most iniquitously unjust variety conceivable, designed to assist English industry at the expense of Scottish. For example, a tax was imposed on all linen exported. Scotland was a linen weaving country; England was not, her staple textile production being of woollens. The result of the impost was the ruining for many years of one of Scotland's main industries.

The Treaty of Union had not been in existence for many years before it had been violated in practically every clause by the English majority who controlled the joint parliament. The laws of Scotland were set aside; the liberties of her church were infringed; her industries were stifled; her courts were subjected to the control of an English assembly.

Says Professor Hume Brown, a historian who believes in the ultimate benefit to Scotland of the Union: "There was not a class in Scotland which had not reason to complain of a breach of the Articles of Union, and to regret that it had ever been accomplished. Clergy, merchants, peers, all in succession had their own special grievances which they were powerless to redress, and from which the only escape, as it seemed, was the dissolution of that Union which had been the cause of all the mischief. To that end, indeed, converged the feelings of all classes in the country."

If only the Stewarts were back again, there would be at least a king with Scottish sympathies, and a chance to get rid of English oppressions. Such was the feeling which quickly spread through a large part of the nation, and which was in a great degree responsible for the two Jacobite risings.

An attempt was made to secure the repeal of the Union by constitutional methods. In 1713, a Bill was introduced in the House of Lords for the dissolution of the inequable partnership, but it was narrowly defeated, by a majority of four votes. It became apparent then, or so it seemed to many, that other means must be adopted.

In 1712, the earl of Mar had written to a correspondent, "If we saw a possibility of getting free of the Union without a civil war, we would have some comfort, but that I am afraid is impossible." That civil war was soon to come, with Mar as the central figure in it.

On the death of Anne, the last of the real Stewarts, and the accession of George I, the situation began to grow serious. A correspondent of Forbes of Culloden wrote to him, "The vanity, insolence, arrogance and madness of the Jacobites is beyond all measure insupportable. I believe they must be let blood." The Hanoverians fully realised the strength of the threat that was made against them. The Habeas Corpus Act and the corresponding Scottish law were suspended. A price of £100,000 was put on the head of the Stewart king in the event of his venturing into Britain, while the more prominent of his adherents were deprived of such offices as they held and put under the strictest watch.

o

There was good enough reason for these precautions, particularly in Scotland, where whole districts were almost entirely against the existing Government. The city of Aberdeen was wholly Jacobite, Ayrshire and Dumfriesshire were seething with disaffection, not from love of James, but from indignation against the invasion of the rights of the Scottish church by the London Parliament. In the Highlands the great majority of the clans were prepared to take the field to bring "the auld Stewarts back again." On various pretexts great numbers of armed Highlanders had assembled on several occasions, and had made no effort to conceal their readiness to support their political principles with the sword.

On the 2nd of August, 1715, the die was cast. The earl of Mar left London on his errand of raising Scotland for the king across the water. Disguised as a workman, and accompanied only by two officers and two servants, all in similar guise, he sailed from the Thames in a coal-boat, and eight days later landed at Elie, in Fife.

Agents had gone ahead of him, to prepare the way, and had got into touch with all the prominent Jacobites among the landed gentry of Scotland, who were invited to attend a great hunting meeting on Mar's estate, a very plausible covering at that time for a huge assembly. The invitation was widely accepted, and on the appointed day a great concourse of noblemen and lairds came together, including the marquis of Huntly, the marquis of Tullibardine, the Earl Marischal, and the earls of Nithsdale, Traquair, Errol, Southesk, Carnwath, Seaforth and Linlithgow. It needed little argument on the part of Mar to persuade them to declare themselves for King James VIII, and to agree to raise his standard openly in the field.

The Government got wind of what was afoot, as they could scarcely help doing, and in nervous alarm passed hurriedly what came to be known as the "Clan Act," by which any landed proprietor guilty of treasonable correspondence with the Stewarts was condemned to forfeit his estates. A special clause made void all entails in favour of children and other heirs. This sweeping measure, which invaded an established principle of Scottish law, had exactly the opposite effect to what was expected of it. Instead of intimidating the Jacobite nobles, it confirmed them in their resolution to be rid of a usurping king who had no respect for their privileges.

On the 6th of September, 1715, the royal standard was raised at Castleton in Braemar, and under it James VIII and III was proclaimed King of Great Britain and Ireland.

Only about sixty persons were present at this formal declaration of war on the house of Hanover. Steps were quickly taken, however, to recruit an army. The Fiery Cross was sent through the Highland glens, and letters were despatched to the various chiefs and noblemen who had an armed following at their command. An interesting light is thrown on to the state of Scotland in the early eighteenth century by a letter, which has been preserved, addressed by Mar to the factor of his estate of Kildrummie. "Particularly," he wrote, "let my own tenants in Kildrummie know that, if they come not forth with their best arms, I will send a party immediately to burn what they shall miss taking from them; and they may believe this not only a threat, but, by all that's sacred, I'll put it in execution, let my loss be what it will."

Throughout the Highlands there was a speedy and hearty response to the appeal. The first clan to appear in arms were the Mackintoshes. Five hundred of them, under Mackintosh of Borlum, opened the campaign by the capture of the important town of Inverness, then, leaving a garrison there, hurried to join Mar. Their example was quickly followed by the other Jacobite tribes of the north and west; and soon there was assembled in . Braemar a force sufficiently strong to begin the march to the south.

About the middle of September Mar's army was at
Dunkeld, where it received a reinforcement of 4000
men from Atholl and Breadalbane. A few days later
the town of Perth was seized. Other burghs had
voluntarily joined the insurrection, the majority of
their citizens being of Stewart sympathies. King James
was proclaimed, amid public rejoicings, at the market
crosses of Aberdeen, Brechin, and Dundee.

Meanwhile an effort was being made by the Jacobites
of the Lowlands to further the cause there. The three
strongest fortresses in Scotland, the castles of Edinburgh,
Stirling, and Dunbarton, were to be seized and held for
King James. Only in Edinburgh was the attempt
actually made. It failed through several unfortunate
circumstances, of which perhaps the chief was that one
of the conspirators could not keep a secret from his
wife.

The duke of Argyll was appointed to the command of
the Hanoverian troops in Scotland. They were few in
number, only about 2000 regulars, made up to almost
4000 by volunteers from Glasgow, Edinburgh and other
towns. Mar's force, by the month of October, had grown
to more than 12,000 men. Argyll was at Stirling,
perhaps the most important strategic point in Scotland.
Mar's troops were assembled at Perth, from which place
he controlled all the eastern counties from the Forth
to the Moray Firth. In the north, the earl of Sutherland
was rumoured to be raising a force for King George,
although little was ever heard of it.

The first move was made by Mar, He put 2500 men
under the command of Mackintosh of Borlum, one of his
most experienced commanders, and had them ferried
across the firth of Forth from Fife to the Lothians,
with the object of marching south to join the Lowland
Jacobites under Viscount Kenmure and the earl of
Derwentwater's band from Northumberland. Mar's idea
was that the joint force should occupy Glasgow, and so
enable him to enclose Argyll in a net; instead of which, it

marched into England, at the instigation of the Northumberland men, and came to disaster at Preston.

Mar himself, with his main body, lingered in Perth until the 10th of November. Then he was impelled to take some definite action by the arrival of news that a large body of Dutch troops were on their way to England and would be sent north to join Argyll at Stirling. Without further delay it was imperative that Argyll should be driven out of his stronghold, and the whole of Scotland occupied by James's men.

Mar's plan was to cross the Forth by a ford near Aberfoyle. Argyll got word of it, and sent an urgent summons to the Government troops in Glasgow, Edinburgh, Kilsyth, and Falkirk to join him at once. On the morning of the 12th, he broke up his camp at Stirling, and marched northward to intercept the rebels. That evening he was near the edge of Sheriffmuir, about two and a half miles to the east of Dunblane, where he decided to await the arrival of his enemies, whose road to the south must take them past the moor.

From Perth, Mar marched by way of Auchterarder, and on the evening of the 12th was at Kinbuck, about two miles from Argyll's position at Sheriffmuir. There the clans spent the night; and in the morning an old peasant woman, sent by the "goodwife of Kippendavie," brought word to them that Argyll's force was close at hand. It was apparent that the hour for the trial of strength had come.

The advantage of numbers was with Mar. He had 8000 men, against Argyll's 3500. That was his only advantage. Argyll was a soldier and a general, reckoned one of the best in the army. Mar was an inexperienced amateur, whose ablest implement was his tongue. Before the battle he made "a very fine speech," which one of his commanders tell us was "the only good action of his life." His political career had been distinguished by a vacillation that was probably unique, even in an age in which the turning of a coat was accounted more a matter of tactics than of treachery. "Bobbing John" was his nick-name.

Sheriffmuir is a broad and almost level plateau on a spur of the Ochils, overlooking Dunblane. What slope there is is so gentle that it could have presented not the slightest difficulty to Mar's troops had an immediate attack been decided on. Yet, in spite of his numerical superiority of more than two to one, that dialectical general hesitated to give the word, and called a council of war instead.

This assembly was not confined to his responsible and more experienced officers, among whom were men who had fought with Marlborough, but was apparently open to any who cared to offer an opinion. At it there was wasted in talk considerable time that might have been more usefully occupied, for, with Highland troops, it mattered little what arguments there might be for delay. The only possible thing was to fight. So said the chiefs of the clans, and, in such an army, their word was the final one. If they had been denied, they would promptly have taken their men off the field and gone home, for each man of them was a law to himself and to the men of his clan. It was inconceivable to their way of thinking, to face an enemy and not to fight him; and especially such an enemy as Argyll. If Mar would not attack the hated Campbell, they would. There was nothing for it but an immediate advance.

The two armies would appear to have started towards each other almost simultaneously, both making for Sheriffmuir. On every side, that hill has a very gentle slope, but a steady one, with no irregularities or eminences rising above the general level. With two bodies of men approaching from opposite directions, therefore, it was impossible for either to see the other until they were almost in contact. The result was that each held a little further to the right than was necessary, so that the right wing of each army outflanked the left of the other.

The battle was devoid of any attempt at tactics. As
soon as they were within sight of their enemies, the
Highlanders began their attack, firing their muskets,
then throwing them away and setting on with the
broadsword. Their right wing overwhelmed Argyll's
left, commanded by General Witham, driving them in
disorder from the field, and pursuing them to Dunblane.
The Master of Sinclair, who fought in this part of the
field, has left a vivid account of it. "The order to attack
being given, the two thousand Highlanders, who were
then drawn up in very good order, ran towards the enemy
in a disorderly manner, always firing some dropping
shots, which drew upon them a general salvo from the
enemy, which began at their left, opposite to us, and ran
to their right. No sooner that begun, the Highlanders
threw themselves flat on their bellies; and, when it
slackened, they started to their feet. Most threw away
their fugies, and, drawing their swords, pierced them
everywhere with an incredible vigour and rapidity, in
four minutes time from their receiving the order to
attack. Not only all in our view and before us turned
their backs, but the five squadrons of dragoons on their
left, commanded by General Witham, went to the right
about, and never looked back until they had got near
Dunblane, about two miles from us."

On Mar's left a different tale was being told. There
it was he who was outflanked. The first onrush of the
Highlanders was steadily received. They were driven
back; and, before they had time to re-form for another
attack, Argyll's cavalry came thundering down on them,
caught them unprepared, and put them to rout, the
duke's infantry taking up the pursuit.

There was now an astonishing position. The right
wing of each army had been completely victorious,
and had driven the enemy from the field, following up
the success by a considerable pursuit. The battlefield
was deserted, save by the dead and wounded. Some
way to the north of it Argyll's men were chasing Mar's;

to the south Mar's men were cutting down the fleeing troops of Argyll. Each right wing was flushed with victory; each left was in disordered flight.

As the old song has it,

> There's some say that we wan,
> And some say that they wan,
> And some say that nane wan at a', man;
> But ae thing I'm sure,
> That at Sherra-muir
> A battle there was, that I saw, man;
> And we ran, and they ran,
> And they ran, and we ran
> But Florence ran fastest of a', man.

Florence was a celebrated horse belonging to the marquis of Huntly, who apparently made good use of his speed that day.

Mar fled to Perth. When Argyll, with his right wing, returned to the field, he found the victorious part of the Highland army occupying a little hill near Kippendavie. There was no inclination, however, on either side to resume the conflict. After staring at their enemies for a little, the Highlanders drew off; and they were allowed to go.

For so brief an encounter, the casualties were heavy. Argyll lost six hundred men, Mar eight hundred, including the earl of Strathmore and the young chief of Clanranald.

Sheriffmuir must be regarded as a drawn battle, but to the Hanoverians it was as good as a victory, for, by preventing Mar's troops from crossing the Forth, it held up the campaign until the arrival of a sufficient number of English and Dutch regiments to give Argyll the superiority of strength which in a few months brought the rebellion to an end without any further fighting.

Towards the end of December, King James ventured to land in Scotland. Early in February, he hurriedly departed again, and Mar went with him. "Everybody else took the road he liked best," and the Fifteen was over.

GLENSHIEL (10th June, 1719).—In 1719, Spain contemplated an invasion of Britain. An important part
of her scheme was to promote a rising in Scotland on
behalf of the Stewarts. In March a large fleet, carrying
5000 soldiers and an immense quantity of arms, sailed
from Cadiz with the purpose of effecting a landing in
England; and at the same time there set out from San
Sebastian two frigates, with Keith, the Earl Marischal,
and three hundred Spanish infantrymen on board.
The fleet was so damaged by a severe storm that it was
compelled to return to Spain; but the two frigates
landed at Lewis early in April. There Keith was joined
by the marquis of Tullibardine and the earl of Seaforth;
but their hopes of a general rising of the Jacobites in
the Highlands were disappointed, for the news had spread
of the abandonment of the Spanish invasion. Less than
a thousand men answered the call. Government troops,
1100 strong, under General Wightman, marched to meet
the rebels and their allies. In Glenshiel, at the head of
Loch Duich, the two forces came into contact, and after
three hours fighting, in which no great losses were
suffered by either side, the Spaniards, on the advice of
the Jacobite leaders, surrendered, and the Highlanders
scattered to their hills.

Prince Charlie's pledge — I'll conquer or die!

PRESTONPANS.

(21st September, 1745.)

AFTER Sheriffmuir, Jacobitism simmered in Scotland for thirty years, before it suddenly boiled up again in 1745. In 1719, there was an abortive attempt at a rising, but it ended suddenly in the little battle of Glenshiel. There was lacking a leader fit to fire the cause of the Stewarts with enthusiasm, as Montrose and Dundee had done. Such a one was found at last, however, and where perhaps he might least have been expected.

James VIII had made three attempts to be a king in fact as well as in name, and had met with little to encourage him. After Glenshiel he had reconciled himself to be content with the pauperism of a pension from a foreign monarch, and to satisfy his longings for a throne with the hollow pretences of his imitation court in France.

Not so his son Charles. That young prince was a man of better mettle than any of his immediate forebears. He was the heir to a crown, and he was ready to fight for his rights. His father's inertia annoyed him. He could not understand how any man with Stewart blood in him could submit to being a puppet, when his own endeavours might make him a king. Better to die, he thought, in a manly attempt at restoring his family's fortunes than to live on the charity of strangers without ever having made that attempt.

His father had apparently abandoned all ambition, so Charles kept his opinions to himself and waited his opportunity. There were loyal men still in plenty in Scotland, he felt sure; and the day would come when he might summon them to the standard of the Stewarts again with bright hopes of happy fortune.

It came, or so it seemed to the sanguine young prince, in the summer of 1745. On the 11th of May of that year, the British army had been soundly beaten by the French at Fontenoy. Its prestige was at a low ebb both abroad and at home. Now, if ever, was the time when the Jacobites in Scotland and England might be expected to take heart from their enemies' misfortunes and make a bold bid against the house of Hanover.

Charles immediately set about his preparations. He found a firm of bankers prepared to stake a considerable sum on his success. From them he borrowed 180,000 livres. Two English merchants in Nantes agreed to lend him ships to carry himself and his munitions to Scotland, the *Elizabeth*, a ship of sixty-four guns, and the *Doutelle*, a brig of eighteen. These were loaded with arms and ammunition; and, with seven companions, the young adventurer embarked on board the *Doutelle* on the 22nd of June.

A few days before, he had written to his father, the first word James had of the project to put him on his throne: "Let what will happen, the stroke is struck, and I have taken a firm resolution to conquer or to die, and stand my ground as long as I shall have a man remaining with me." A trifle turgid, but the writer was only twenty-four.

The little expedition had scarcely sailed when it came very near to disaster. Off Ushant it fell in with a British man-of-war, the *Lion*, and, in an engagement lasting for several hours, the *Elizabeth*, although she had the best of the fight, was so badly damaged that she had to make her way back to France. The *Doutelle* continued her voyage. On the 23rd of July, she reached Eriska in the Hebrides. Two days later she crossed to the mainland, where Charles landed on Scottish soil at Lochnanuagh, and his most prominent adherents among the Highland chiefs were summoned to attend him.

None of them had any enthusiasm for the adventure of a rising, in which they could see small hope of success.

They had been taken unawares, with no preparations made; and the prince had brought only a scanty store of munitions with him, and not a single man of the French troops that all were agreed would be needed to help in driving King George off the throne and his army into the sea. It was a cold douche for the ardent spirit of the Young Chevalier the reception he met with at Lochnanuagh. He might readily have been pardoned if he had turned tail and gone dejectedly back to France. But, instead, he sent away the *Doutelle*, and announced that he was in Scotland and there he would remain, whatever fortune might be in store for him. His brave demeanour worked on the hearts of the Highlanders as no argument could have done.

The first man to declare himself ready to fight for his king, come what might, was Macdonald of Kinloch Moidart. Then came Donald Cameron, "the gentle Lochiel." I will share the fate of my prince," he said, "and so shall every man over whom nature or fortune has given me any power." Within a few days Glengarry and Clanranald, Macdonald of Keppoch and Stewart of Ardshiel had pledged themselves to the cause.

The first gathering of the clans was arranged for the 10th of August. It was to be at Glenfinnan, a lonely spot at the head of Loch Shiel. On the appointed day, Charles, with a few attendants, was early at the meeting-place. The glen was empty; not a man was there to greet him; in place of the welcoming shouts of loyal clansmen, there were only the cries of the gulls. For two hours the prince sat in a little hovel on the seashore, wrapt in thoughts that cannot have been comforting. Then suddenly the stillness was broken by the sound of the pipes, and seven hundred Camerons came swinging down the glen, their chief at the head of them, claymores buckled at their sides, their tartans bright in the sunshine. His gloom dispersed by their brave array, Charles hurried to meet them.

The standard of James VIII was unfurled by the

duke of Atholl (marquis of Tullibardine), and beneath its folds the prince proclaimed his intention of winning back for his race the throne of Britain. He had come to Scotland because there he could be assured of finding brave men, "fired with the noble example of their predecessors, and jealous of their own and their country's honour, to join with him in so glorious an enterprise." He had no doubt of "bringing the affair to a happy issue."

Only the Camerons were at this simple ceremony. It was scarcely over, however, when Keppoch arrived with three hundred of his Macdonalds; and hard on their heels came a party of Macleods, "who had disclaimed their chief." The little army amounted to about a thousand men. It had thrown a challenge to the whole military force of Britain.

The Government troops then in Scotland consisted of the 6th, 44th, and 47th regiments of foot, and Gardener's and Hamilton's regiments of dragoons. The earl of Loudon's Highland regiment was in active process of being raised. The whole force was under the orders of Sir John Cope, a parade-ground soldier, with an expert knowledge of pipe-clay and button polish, but completely devoid of intelligence and resource, the type of man who in peace time rises to high command in the British army and is responsible for the disasters which almost invariably mark the beginning of a British campaign.

Prince Charles had not been many days in Scotland when Cope learned the fact, communicated to him, by way of Duncan Forbes of Culloden, by Macleod of Macleod, the chief who had outraged the feelings of his clansmen by refusing to take the field with them for their rightful king. Cope notified the War Office of his intention "to march his troops into the Highlands, to seek out the rebels, and try to check their progress," the last phrase scarcely the words of a general with a strong conviction of his own ability. On the 20th of

August he left Stirling, with twenty-five companies of foot and several guns. Skilfully avoiding the rebels, he reached the shelter of Inverness on the 29th, leaving the road to the south freely open to Charles's Highlanders.

Charles had left Glenfinnan on the 21st. He went first to Glengarry, where he was joined by six hundred Macdonalds and two hundred of the ever-loyal Stewarts of Appin. Entering Perthshire, he made for Lude, the seat of the chief of the Robertsons. On the 4th of September he occupied the city of Perth. Here the Macgregors and a section of the Robertsons came to offer their allegiance, also a considerable number of influential gentlemen, of whom the most notable was Lord George Murray, brother of the duke of Atholl, the man who was soon to shew himself the most able leader in the Jacobite army.

Meantime, Cope had apparently awakened to the danger which he had allowed to develop, and realised that the Highlanders were marching on Edinburgh, which they would find an easy prey. He decided to make across country for Aberdeen, and secure transports there to convey his troops to the south, in the hope that they would be in time to save the capital.

This was reported to Charles, who was thus confronted with an important choice between two alternatives, to go north and intercept Cope, or to ignore him and hurry on to Edinburgh. As time was of the utmost importance the latter course was decided on.

On the 13th of September, the Highlanders crossed the Forth by the Fords of Frew. Two days later they were at Linlithgow, and on the following afternoon within sight of Edinburgh. Gardener's dragoons, who had accompanied them, at a safe distance, during the past few days' march, made no attempt at opposition, and, on the morning of the 17th of September, 1745, Prince Charles Edward Stewart entered the capital of his fathers.

He is described by Home, who saw him there. "He

was in the prime of youth, tall and handsome, of a fair complexion; he had a light-coloured periwig with his own hair combed over the front; he wore the Highland dress, that is, a tartan short coat without the plaid, a blue bonnet on his head, and on his breast the star of the order of St. Andrew."

At noon King James was proclaimed at the Mercat Cross of Edinburgh; and for two days his son held royal state in Holyrood. Then came the news that Cope had landed his army at Dunbar and was hurrying to give battle.

On the 20th the Government troops had taken up a position across the Edinburgh-Dunbar road, between Preston and Tranent, facing towards Edinburgh.

By nine o'clock that morning Charles's army was assembled at Duddingston and eager for the approaching battle. Before they marched, the prince spoke to his officers. "Gentlemen," he said, "I have flung away the scabbard. With God's assistance, I do not doubt of making you a free and happy people."

Asked by Charles how the men were likely to behave when faced by the enemy, Macdonald of Keppoch replied that that was hard to tell, for few or none of the "private men" had ever seen a battle. The chiefs and their kin, however, would certainly be in the midst of the Englishmen, and he ventured to be sure that wherever they were their men would not be far away from them.

Cope had chosen to draw up his troops on exactly the kind of ground that would appeal to a pipe-clay general, the comparatively level plain bordering the firth, with no regard to the fact that on the south it was closely commanded by a ridge running parallel with the sea. The Highlanders were not slow to profit from his carelessness.

They had expected, as intelligent men would, to find their opponent strongly posted on the higher ground, and could scarcely believe their good fortune when they discovered that he had utterly neglected it and had

contented himself with the seaboard. Lord George
Murray, who was in command of the van, saw his
opportunity, and quickly seized it, leading the Camerons
up on to the high ground towards Tranent, while the
rest of the army followed. The first knowledge that
Cope had of the nearness of his foes was when he saw
them lining the ridge above him.

He must have been intensely annoyed that they had
so far forgotten the principles of good sportsmanship,
to be expected in decent enemies, as to take him at a
disadvantage, instead of marching up to him in nice
parade order. Fortunately he was on ground not too
different from a barrack square; so, smartly manoeuvring
his line, he changed its front towards the south, facing
the men on the ridge. Then he waited developments,
having done all he could think of.

The Highlanders were in no particular hurry. They
held a strong position, and their enemies shewed no
disposition to attempt to push them off it, so there was
time to consider the situation. To attack straight
downhill would have been both difficult and dangerous,
for some marshy ground and a number of dykes and
walls lay between them and the red-coats. A better
plan must be discovered, once the lie of the land had been
thoroughly investigated.

All afternoon the two armies faced each other, and
when night came they lay down where they had stood.
Cope had the village of Cockenzie behind him; on his
right was the village of Preston, occupied by five hundred
of Charles's men, under Lord Nairn; in front of him a
deep ditch cut across the long strip of marsh at the edge
of the plain. On this ditch it was that he put his main
reliance for defence; and indeed it was a formidable
obstacle, the main reason for the delay in the Highlanders'
attack. His flanks were guarded by his two regiments
of cavalry, Gardener's men near Preston, Hamilton's
on the left. The clans were disposed along the ridge
on each side of Tranent. There they lay in absolute

darkness and strictly enforced silence, in contrast to the blazing camp-fires and the loud challenges of sentries on the plain below them. It might have been Charles and not Cope who was the trained general, the ragged clans not the gorgeted red-coats who were the seasoned troops.

After dark the prince held a council of his officers. The dangers of the marsh and the ditch were fully realised, and it was decided that before daybreak the bulk of the army should be concentrated to the east of Tranent, where the ground seemed to be more favourable for an attack. That had not long been agreed on, however, when there was brought to Lord George Murray a young volunteer who claimed to know the neighbourhood well and offered to lead the way to a little valley by which might be reached the level ground to the east of Cope's position, thus allowing an attack on his left flank. The suggestion was communicated to Charles and his principal officers, and immediately approved of.

Lord Nairn's party was brought in from Preston, and at three o'clock in the morning, in absolute silence, the whole army moved along the ridge. Their guide was as good as his word. Before daybreak the Highlanders were forming up in two lines on Cope's left. In front were the Macdonalds, in their place of honour on the right, the Camerons and Appin Stewarts on the left, and the duke of Perth's regiment with the Macgregors in the centre. The second line was drawn up fifty yards behind the front one; it consisted of the Atholl men, the Robertsons, the Maclachlans and the Macdonalds of Glencoe. The prince's desire had been to put himself in the centre of the first rank of his men, as his ancestor had done at Flodden; but he was persuaded that such a risk would be unjustifiable. With his staff, he took his place midway between the two lines.

As the Highlanders were forming, they were discovered by some cavalry videttes of Cope's, who immediately gave the alarm. The troops were called to arms, and a

P

hurried and only partly successful attempt was made to
swing round their line to the east, to meet the onrush of
the clans that was now obviously close at hand.

Just as the sun was beginning to struggle through the
morning mist, the Highland army began its advance,
running swiftly forward over the stubble with which
the ground was covered, each man bending low as he
ran, so that the targe he held in front of him might shield
the more of his body from the Sassenach musket-balls.
The tactics were to be the same as at Killiecrankie.
Not a shot would be fired from the advancing line until
the range was only a few yards; then the muskets would
be thrown away and the claymores would do their office.

Racing ahead of the rest of the line, the Camerons were
the first to reach the enemy.   It was Gardener's dragoons
they encountered.   That gallant regiment was so terrified
by the sight of the tartans and the flashing claymores
that it reeled back at the first impact, then wheeled
round and fled for Edinburgh, leaving its commander
to face the enemy without a man by his side.   Hamilton's
dragoons, on Cope's other flank, did not even wait to
meet the Macdonalds who were coming at them, but
swung round their horses, and galloped away without
firing a carbine or drawing a sabre.

Cope's infantry discharged a single unsteady volley,
then broke in panic as the clans rushed through their
ranks.   Only one small group, rallied round Colonel
Gardener, made any show of resistance, fighting with
their backs to a wall until their leader was slain.   The
others had thrown down their weapons and run for their
lives the moment the first of the claymores were among
them.

Reliable witnesses attested that the actual battle lasted
for four minutes.   It was probably less; for the second
line of the Highlanders, only fifty yards behind the front
one, was never engaged, but arrived only in time to join
in the pursuit of the fleeing red-coats.

Cope had had about 2000 men. All his dragoons, thanks

The surprise dawn charge of the Highlanders

*The Prince moves among the casualties
after the battle*

to their cowardice, escaped. Of his infantry, 400 were slain, most of them as they fled, 700 were made prisoners, and less than 200 managed to get away. The Highlanders had thirty men killed and about seventy wounded.

After the battle, the victors displayed a spirit of humanity which is in striking contrast to the conduct of their enemies when, seven months later, the positions were reversed. Prince Charles and Lord George Murray exerted themselves to their utmost to provide relief for the sufferings of the wounded, and in this they had the willing support of the clansmen, the men supposed to be savages. One of Clanranald's officers records in his memoirs, "Whatever notion our Low-country people may entertain of the Highlanders, I can attest they gave many proofs this day of their humanity and mercy. Not only did I often hear our common clansmen ask the soldiers if they wanted quarter, and not only did we, the officers, exert our utmost pains to save those who were stubborn, or who could not make themselves understood, but I saw some of our private men, after the battle, run to Port Seton for ale and other liquors to support the wounded. As one proof for all, of my own particular observation, I saw a Highlander carefully, and with patient kindness, carry a poor wounded soldier on his back into a house, where he left him, with a sixpence to pay his charges. In all this, we followed not only the dictates of humanity but also the orders of our prince."

On the evening of the battle, Cope reached Coldstream, forty miles away; good running! Next day he found shelter in Berwick, where old Lord Mark Kerr exclaimed: "Good God! I have seen some battles, heard of many, but never before of the first news of defeat being brought by the general officers."

Originally styled the battle of Preston, from the little village of that name in whose neighbourhood it was fought, the engagement has now come to be known by the more modern title of Prestonpans. By the Jacobites it was always referred to as the battle of Gladsmuir.

Through blinding rain the enemies faced each other

FALKIRK (II).

(17th January, 1746.)

THE news of Cope's defeat at Preston spread like wild-fire through Scotland, heartening the Jacobites and casting dismay over their enemies. The English general became a figure-of-fun for the rhymesters of the victorious party.

> When Johnnie Cope to Dunbar came,
> They speered at him, "Where's a' your men?"
> "The deil confound me gin I ken,
> For I left them a' i' the morning."

> "Now, Johnnie, troth ye werena blate,
> To come wi' the news o' your ain defeat,
> And leave your men in sic a strait
> So early i' the morning."

> "I' faith," quo' Johnnie, "I got a fleg
> Wi' their claymores and philabegs;
> If I face them again, deil break my legs!
> So I wish you a very gude morning."

Charles had in his hands the whole of Scotland, with the exception of the fortresses, of which the chief were the castles of Stirling and Edinburgh. His fortunes, so little promising when, only a few weeks before, he landed from the *Doutelle*, had undergone a brilliant change. He was the feted leader of a victorious army. Each day brought new adherents, eager to have their share in the Stewart triumph. The white cockade, so long worn only in secret gatherings, was flaunted in the streets of every town in Scotland; and white breast-knots were even more common than cockades.

Recruits came pouring in, though mostly from the loyal north. Lord Ogilvie, the eldest son of the earl of Airlie, brought six hundred men, his father's tenants, most of them of his own name. Gordon of Glenbucket appeared at the head of four hundred men from the shires of Aberdeen and Banff, while Lord Pitsligo led in a numerous body of cavalry, gentlemen and their servants, from the same counties, all well mounted and well armed. Lord Lewis Gordon, the brother of the duke, came and kissed the prince's hand, and held out hope of the rising of the whole of his people. In smaller numbers parties came from other clans in the north and west, so that, by the end of October, Charles's army had increased to at least five thousand men, more than double the number of those who scattered the Hanoverian regiments at Gladsmuir.

In the Lowlands there was little but disappointment for the recruiters. There were plenty to cry huzza for King James, but few to attach themselves to his standard. If Scotland was to regain her freedom and the Stewarts their throne, it must be by the claymores of the Highlanders.

Apart from a few gentlemen of noble families. who brought no more than their body-servants with them, the Low-country supplied only a handful of fighting men to the prince. A useful contribution, however, was reluctantly made by the burghs of the south. which were forced to comply with demands for food and equipment and money. Edinburgh contributed goods to such value as to entail the infliction of a rate of half-a-crown on the pound of assessed rental. Glasgow was mulcted of £5500; and smaller towns paid lesser sums in proportion to their size.

For six weeks Charles held court in Holyroodhouse. while his army was being recruited and sundry matters put in order. All the time, he was impatient to be over the Border and carry the war into England, where he entertained the highest hopes of a warm reception from a loyal people. His principal advisers had no such ideal. They felt that they could hold Scotland for their king. and it was with Scotland alone that they were concerned. German George might keep England, for all that they cared. If the English people wished the Stewarts back to London, they must go about the business themselves.

Charles argued strongly, however—he was not in a position to command—and eventually he had his way. That was perhaps the first of his misfortunes. If he had consented to devote himself to keeping Scotland, which he had won so easily, there is a great possibility that he would have succeeded. To invade England with Scottish troops was only to force his enemies to continue a war in which they were bound in the end to be victorious.

On the 1st of November the ill-fated march to England began. It lasted until the 4th of December, on which day Derby was reached by a disappointed army which had collected scarcely a couple of hundred recruits among the Jacobites of the north and west of England. Two days later began the retreat, the foot-weary march back to Scotland, with Cumberland's well-mounted dragoons constantly harassing the rear-guard and Wade's cavalry on the flank. Carlisle was reached on the 19th of December, and Glasgow a week later. On the 6th of January, the army was digging trenches outside of Stirling, with the object of investing that town and reducing the castle.

In spite of the failure of the English adventure, the situation in Scotland was found to have distinctly improved during the previous two months. Lord Lewis Gordon had raised his clan; the Frasers had taken the field under the Master of Lovat; and considerable bodies of Mackintoshes, Mackenzies and Farquharsons had taken the white cockade; while at last a body of troops, eight hundred strong, had come from France. With these reinforcements, Charles's army now amounted to eight thousand men, the greatest strength that it had ever had.

In command of the Government troops in Scotland, Cope had been succeeded by General Hawley, an officer with no gift for leadership beyond a blind confidence in the staunchness of his soldiers. He had almost eight thousand of them, of whom thirteen hundred were cavalry, and was in daily expectation of the arrival of six thousand Hessians in the Forth.

Deciding to relieve Stirling, Hawley marched his troops to Falkirk, which he reached on the 16th. The following day he was joined by over a thousand Campbells, a clan which, for some reason of its own, always chose to side with the enemies of its neighbours.

Lord George Murray was well familiar with the character of his Highlanders. Knowing that they were infinitely better fitted for attack than for defence, he strongly urged that, instead of waiting for Hawley to come to Stirling, the Jacobite army should take up the offensive. In this, Charles and all his officers agreed; so the duke of Perth, with twelve hundred men, was left to continue the investment of Stirling, while the others marched to the Plean Moor, about seven miles from Falkirk.

This was on the morning of the 17th. General Hawley was at the time in perhaps the last place and occupation in which an English officer might have been expected to be discovered. He was drinking tea with Lady Kilmarnock in Callendar House. The countess had asked him to breakfast, and he had willingly accepted the invitation, although he was well aware that the lady's husband was one of the principal officers of the rebel army, and she herself an ardent Jacobite.

Towards mid-day reports reached the English camp that the Highlanders were at Plean and were advancing on Falkirk. The news was sent to Hawley; but he was finding himself very comfortable in Callendar House with his charming hostess; so he gave orders for the men to put on their accoutrements, and himself remained where he was.

Between one and two o'clock it was discovered that a body of Highland infantry had crossed the Carron near Dunipace, and it became obvious that an attack was imminent. The officers on duty formed up the men in front of the camp, and sent an urgent message to Hawley, who presently arrived, bare-headed and flustered.

Mindful of Gladsmuir, Charles was making for a stretch of rising ground, known as Falkirk Muir, which overlooked the English camp. This manoeuvre was detected, and Hawley resolved that he would not make the same error as Cope had done. Hurriedly ordering his cavalry to make for the crest of the hill, he led his infantry after them, and left his artillery to follow at the best pace they could make. The dragoons galloped off with sabres drawn. The footmen, their bayonets plugged into their muskets, plodded in their wake. The ten guns went lumbering away behind the teams of a band of Falkirk carters, who, with no enthusiasm for the service of George of Hanover, promptly bogged them in a marsh, then cut the traces and went quietly home.

Charles, in the meantime, had been ascending the other slope of the moor. Soon it became a race for the top, and the clans won, with the Macgregors at the head of them. The Highlanders drew up in two lines, about two hundred paces apart, on the topmost ridge, and the English dragoons, when they arrived, were forced to content themselves with lower ground, where presently they were joined by their comrades on foot.

The two armies were roughly equal in size, about eight thousand men apiece. Neither had any artillery, as Charles had left his guns at Stirling; but Hawley had an immense superiority in cavalry, on which he based his confidence of victory.

A storm had come on, and through blinding rain the enemies faced each other. In the front line of the Highlanders, commanded by Murray, were the Macgregors, the Macdonalds of Keppoch, Clanranald's men, Glengarry's men, the Appin Stewarts, the Camerons, the Frasers, and the Macphersons. Behind them were the Atholl men, the Ogilvies, the Gordons, the Farquharsons, Cromarty's men, and the French troops. With his small body of horse, the prince was in the rear of the second line. Hawley's force was assembled in two lines also, five regular regiments in each, with the Campbells and the Glasgow regiment of militia as reserve. Three of Hawley's regiments on the right outflanked the prince's left, a fact which was to have an important bearing on the issue of the day. The dragoons were in front, and to the left, of the first line of foot.

It was nearly four o'clock, and darkness was coming on under the overcast sky, when the battle began with a cavalry charge of the whole three regiments of dragoons, which was expected by the English commander to sweep the Highlanders off their ground and down the hill. To the utter astonishment of the horsemen, they were received with unshaken steadiness by the Macgregors and Macdonalds, against whom their attack had been directed. As ordered by Murray, the clans held their fire until their enemies were within pistol-shot. Then a volley crashed out from their whole line at almost point-blank range, and in an instant the dragoons were broken. As they had done at Preston, they wheeled their horses and fled for their lives, galloping through their own infantry in their panic. One single troop, under Colonel Whitney, made a show of fight, breaking into the ranks of the Highlanders, but their horses were dirked and every man of them was slain or captured. Hawley's cavalry, on which he had put such reliance, had melted away in a moment.

This was poor heartening for the infantry, who were now ordered forward. The Highlanders came to meet them, elated by their easy success over the dragoons; but the red-coats had no stomach for their job. Their military ardour thoroughly damped by the drenching rain and the spectacle of the fleeing cavalry, they broke and ran before the clans had come within reach of them, streaming in a terror-stricken mob back to Falkirk, and carrying their general with them.

It would have been Gladsmuir over again but for one

circumstance. The three regiments on Hawley's right, which outflanked the clans, kept their ground, as it was very easy for them to do with no thirsting claymores flashing down on them. They poured a volley into the flank of the charging line of Highlanders, who, thinking an ambush had been laid for them, drew back to their former ground to await developments. The three regiments then retired in good order, while, uncertain what to do, the victorious clans remained still on the battlefield. The result was that practically the whole of Hawley's force got safely through Falkirk and on to the road for Edinburgh. There was no pursuit, probably from Charles's lack of cavalry.

The fleeing troops spent the night in Linlithgow, where the dragoons completed their day's work by firing the palace. Next day Hawley reached Edinburgh, having put twenty-six miles between himself and his enemies. Before leaving that city, he had erected two gibbets on which he proposed to hang the principal rebels whom he should bring back from his victory. He used them now to string up a number of his own dragoons, and no one could grudge him that satisfaction.

The losses at Falkirk were small on both sides, for the Government troops did not wait on the field long enough either to inflict damage on their opponents or to suffer casualties themselves. Charles had thirty-two men killed and 120 wounded. Hawley confessed to losing 280 including prisoners, but as the statement occurs in the middle of a blustering apology for his disgrace the number is probably an under estimate.

How brave clansmen were massacred by butchers

CULLODEN.

(16th April, 1746.)

For a fortnight after his victory at Falkirk, Charles continued the siege of Stirling Castle. There was no sign, however, of weakening on the part of the defenders of that fortress, and time became pressing. The fugitive Hanoverian regiments had been pulled together again, and others had joined them; while, in place of Hawley, the command of the Government forces in Scotland had passed to the brutish and entirely ruthless son of King George, the duke of Cumberland, a man of recent experience in war who had not disgraced himself at Fontenoy. In the next battle there would be a stronger enemy under an abler leader than at Preston or Falkirk.

These facts would probably have caused little perturbation to Charles and his officers but for a greater danger that confronted them. Five months had passed since the first gathering at Glenfinnan. Many of the men had been in the field almost the whole of that time, a long period for a Highland army to hold together. The clans were becoming restless, and already, on one pretext and another, groups were slipping away to their homes. They did not look on this in any way as desertion, for they were very willing to return again whenever their private affairs had been attended to. They were not regular soldiers. They knew little of military discipline; and can be pardoned for a reluctance to remain too long away from the crofts on which their future livelihood depended. The fields would require to be tilled for the spring sowing, and there would be cattle to be seen to.

The chiefs knew their men, and urged Charles to leave Stirling and retire into the Highlands. The prince yielded, though with regret, to the counsel of his advisers; and on the 1st of February the Highland army started for the north.

The first objective was Inverness, which was occupied for the Government by the earl of Loudon with the regiment of irregulars he had raised. They were not a very determined band, for, on the first rumour of Charles's approach, they decided that discretion was better than valour and scampered off to the Black Isle. On the 20th of February, Charles entered the town. A month later, Loudon's force, which had been pursued into Sutherland, was dispersed with little difficulty.

The Jacobites had other successes in the north-west. By the early days of March, both Fort George and Fort Augustus had fallen into their hands. Fort William was more difficult. Garrisoned by Guise's regiment, it resisted all attempts at capture until it was relieved by Cumberland after his victory at Culloden.

While the Highlanders were thus occupied with the northern fortresses, the Hanoverian prince had collected a considerable force, and was carefully making his plans for the decisive action which would put an end to the rebellion. On the 25th of February he was at Aberdeen, where he remained for six weeks, in no hurry to make a move until he felt that he was ready. On the 8th of April he had his arrangements completed, and set out for the west. Three days later he came to Cullen, where the duke of Perth was stationed with a strong body of Highlanders, who, however, withdrew without offering any resistance, and Cumberland passed on to Nairn, which he reached on the 14th.

Charles was at Culloden, seven miles from Inverness and near the edge of Drummossie Moor, when he learned that Cumberland was now close at hand. Messengers were sent hot-foot to all his scattered detachments, urging them to join the prince immediately, as an engagement with the enemy was imminent. To assemble the whole Jacobite army was impossible; so many parties were on special duties at a considerable distance from the main body, Lord Cromarty, for example, with the Macgregors, the Mackinnons and the Mackenzies, being still in the wilds of Sutherland watching the remnants of the earl of Loudon's force. By the morning of the 15th April, however, all the clans which were within reach were gathered at Culloden.

Charles was faced now with the most difficult problem of his campaign, to fight or to retire to the shelter of the hills until he could meet his enemies with the strongest force at his command. He had a different opponent now from Cope and Hawley, and he was fully aware of it. Cumberland had perhaps no particular genius, but he had a cool head, which could be depended on in battle, unquestioned courage and determined energy. What was equally important, he had with him the best troops in his father's service, men tried in war on the Continent. He had left Edinburgh with three regiments of horse and fourteen battalions of foot, 14,000 men in all, and although he had stationed two of his battalions of Hessian infantry at Stirling and four at Perth, to guard his rear, he had still at his disposal a force which was considerably larger than Charles's and infinitely better equipped.

Although Lord George Murray had exclaimed, on hearing that the Hanoverians had crossed the Spey, "The more of the Elector's men come over, the fewer there will be to return!" he was by no means confident as to the issue of an immediate encounter with them. The best promise of success seemed to lie in a surprise attack, and that was the plan which was ultimately agreed on.

The 15th of April was Cumberland's birthday, and there was good reason for hoping that "the red-coats would all be drunk." These fortunate soldiers had, in fact, received that day a generous issue of brandy with which to drink to their commander's health, and they had doubtless found further supplies in the numerous public-houses of Nairn, so the reasoning of the Jacobite leaders was sufficiently sound. Their plan was to approach Cumberland's camp in absolute silence in the dead of night, and make their attack while the majority of their enemies were asleep and many of them probably too fuddled to make any effective resistance. No fire-arms were to be used, but only dirk and claymore. In two parties, approaching from different quarters, the Highlanders were to rush on the sleeping camp, over-power the sentries, cut down the tents so as to entangle their occupants among the ropes and canvas, and then win a speedy victory with their broadswords.

At eight o'clock in the evening the column set off, Lord George Murray in command of the vanguard, the prince at the head of the main body. They hoped to reach their objective soon after midnight, a liberal allowance of time under ordinary circumstances, for it was only some nine miles away. There were unthought of difficulties, however. The men were in no condition for hard marching, for they were more than half starved: on short rations for weeks, that day they had had only one tiny bannock of the coarsest bread apiece. Then the pitch darkness of the night, so encouraging in one way to the venture, was in another the gravest obstacle. The road had to be avoided, for obvious reasons; and the march was over broken ground, heather and bog, a difficult enough route in daylight, ten times more so in the dark. The men could do no more than stumble along at the sorriest pace, and at two o'clock in the morning the van had still three miles to go. The prince and the rest of the men were far in the rear and out of touch.

All idea of surprise had to be abandoned, for it would certainly be daylight before the whole body could possibly be assembled within striking distance of the Hanoverian camp. Murray therefore called his officers together, and, since Charles could not be consulted, took on himself the responsibility of ordering a retiral.

May 1746. *The order of battle on Culloden moor, April 16.* 217

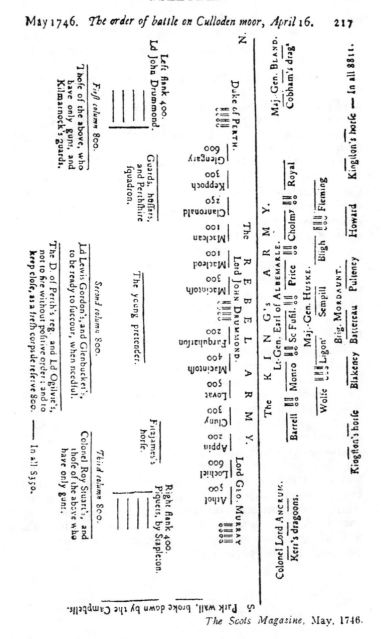

N

Maj.-Gen. BLAND.
Cobham's drag⁵

Kingſton's horſe — In all 8811.

Duke of PERTH.

Left flank 400.
Ld John Drummond.

Thoſe of the above, who have only guns, and Kilmarnock's guards.

Firſt column 800.

Guards, huſſars, and Perthſhire ſquadron.

600 Glengary
300 Keppoch
250 Clanronald
100 Maclean

The REBEL ARMY.

Lord JOHN DRUMMOND.

100 Macleod
300 Macintoſh

The young pretender.

200 Farquharſon
400 Macintoſh
500 Lovat
300 Cluny
200 Appin
600 Lochiel
500 Athol

Ld Lewis Gordon's, and Glenbucket's, to be ready to ſuccour, when needful.

The D. of Perth's reg. and Ld Ogilvie's, not to fire without poſitive order ; and to keep cloſe, as a freſh corps de reſerve 800.

Second column 800.

Fitzjame's horſe.

Third column 800.

Colonel Roy Stuart's, and thoſe of the above who have only guns.

Right flank 400.
Piquets, by Stapleton.

—— In all 5350.

The KING's ARMY.

Lt.-Gen. Earl of ALBEMARLE.

Royal ‖‖ Cholmy ‖‖ Price ‖‖ Sc Fuſil. ‖‖ Monro ‖‖ Barrell ‖‖

Fleming ‖‖‖ Bligh ‖‖‖ Sempill ‖‖‖ Ligon ‖‖‖ Wolfe ‖‖‖

Maj.-Gen. HUSKE.

Brig. MORDAUNT.

Howard Pulteney Battereau Blakeney Kingſton's horſe

Colonel Lord ANCRUM.
Ker's dragoons.

Lord Gco. MURRAY.

At seven o'clock in the morning, weary and dispirited, the clansmen were back at Culloden, where, without a bite to eat, they threw themselves down to sleep on the heather.

At eleven o'clock in the forenoon the alarm was raised. Across the wide stretch of Drummossie Moor, Cumberland's troops could be seen approaching. There was a hurried call to arms and some argument as to whether to stand or to retreat. Charles was all for fighting, and he had his way.

Quickly the Highland army was drawn up on the moor, facing the oncoming columns of Cumberland. As usual there were two lines. In the front, from right to left, were the following clan regiments, the Atholl men, the Camerons, the Appin Stewarts, the Macphersons, the Frasers, the Mackintoshes, the Farquharsons, the Macleods, the Macleans, Clanranald's Macdonalds, Keppoch's Macdonalds and Glengarry's Macdonells. Two guns were placed on each flank and two in the centre of the line. In the second line, a sadly meagre one, were Lord Ogilvie's regiment, Lord Lewis Gordon's, the duke of Perth's, the Irish and the French. On the flanks, the small troops of horsemen were formed.

There was still more than a mile of moor between his regiments and the waiting clans, when Cumberland halted his troops and formed them in position for battle. The infantry were in three lines, six battalions in the first, five in the second and four in the third. They were so arranged that the centre of a battalion in the second line was immediately in rear of the junction of each two in front, and similarly with the third. They were built together, in short, like bricks in a wall, a very strong formation for the tactics of the period. Between each two infantry units in the front line were two guns, while three more were on each flank of the second. On each flank of the infantry was a regiment of cavalry, and a third one was in reserve in rear. The Campbells provided the baggage-guard.

There has been considerable doubt as to the relative
strengths of the two armies. A contemporary account
of the battle, in the *Scots Magazine* of May 1746, gives
them each between 8000 and 9000 men. This is undoubtedly wrong, absurdly so in the case of the prince's
force. The usual estimate allows Cumberland 10,000,
and Charles 5000, but this also is unlikely to be correct.
Cumberland's "parade state" for the day has been
preserved; it shews him to have had, in regular troops,
335 officers and 6076 other ranks. To these must be
added the Campbells and other auxiliaries, making a
total of perhaps 7500. There is no record of the numbers
on the other side, but there is sufficient evidence for a
conclusion that they cannot have amounted to more than
between 3000 and 4000.

Of the physical condition of the two forces it is easier
to make an accurate comparison. Cumberland's men
had had a night's rest and a full breakfast, and had
marched only some eight miles along a good road.
Charles's Highlanders were famished, and exhausted
after a whole night of tramping over marsh and moor.

When he had formed his lines, the duke ordered his
regiments forward again. They continued to advance
until they were within five hundred yards of the clans;
then they were halted, and a slight re-arrangement was
made which had a vital effect on the fortunes of the battle.
Wolfe's regiment, which had been on the left of the second
line, was brought forward and placed at an angle to the
left of the first one, so as to enfilade any attack by the
Highlanders.

The action began about one o'clock in the afternoon.
It was opened by Charles's artillery with a cannonade
which did very little harm. The enemy's guns replied,
with much greater effect, cutting lanes through the
ranks of the Highlanders.

The morning had been fine, with the sun shining. As
the battle commenced it began suddenly to rain, and
turned shortly to a storm of sleet and snow, which drove

Q

into the faces of the clansmen as they stood under the galling fire of the English guns, and added every minute to their impatience to come to close quarters with the enemy. The prince realised that his men could not long be held back, and sent a message to Murray ordering an advance. The messenger was killed on the way, but his errand had become needless, for the clans had broken already from the leash.

The first to charge were the Mackintoshes. Angered beyond endurance by the havoc that was being wrought by the enemy's guns, they leapt from their place in the centre of the line, rushed in headlong fury across the moor, and threw themselves among the foremost ranks of the Englishmen. Such an example could have but one effect on the other clans. In a moment the whole front was racing madly forward through the driving sleet.

Every musket in Cumberland's foremost line blazed at the charging Highlanders; the cannon were volleying grape-shot, now at point-blank range: but not for an instant did the clans waver, even when Wolfe's men caught them in enfilade fire. On they came, an avalanche of tartan and steel, each claymore poised for its slash at an English breast, every dirk gripped firm in a hand that would show no mercy when the point was at an enemy's throat.

No troops, not even the staunchest, could have stopped that first wild onrush of the clans. It carried them clear through the foremost line of Cumberland's regiments, scattering the redcoat soldiers like straws in the wind as the claymores flashed and fell. Then on they went again, and the second line was pierced in places. But the third line stood firm, with bayonets levelled, and slew every man who reached it.

The impetus of their onslaught spent, the survivors of the Highlanders fell back again like a receding wave; and, as they were rallying to launch another attack, they were mowed down in heaps by the musket and cannon fire that beset them both in front and on the flank. They made an attempt to advance, were brought to a standstill, then broke and fled.

Now the English dragoons came thundering forward. They were met, and thrown back, by the prince's reserves, the Irish and the Gordons in particular making a resolute stand. But the horsemen wheeled and came on again—and the battle was over. It was with the greatest difficulty—by force, it was even said—that the prince was persuaded to leave the field on which his hopes had been shattered.

It would have been well for the honour of British arms if the story could have ended here; but all must be told. When the battle was over, the worst slaughter began. The victorious troops roamed over the battlefield, bayoneting in cold blood every wounded Highlander who lay helpless at their feet, while the dragoons cut down every fugitive they could come up with, with no offer of quarter, so that for four miles the road to Inverness was strewn with mangled corpses. This is no Jacobite invention. In the *Scots Magazine* for April, 1746, there are extracts from letters written by officers of Cumberland's army immediately after the battle. One man relates that "they (the Highlanders) made a short pause, retreated a little, and then, turning short round fled with the utmost precipitation. But by this time our horse and dragoons had closed in upon them from both wings, and then followed a general carnage. *The moor was covered with blood; and our men, what with killing the enemy, dabbling their feet in the blood, and splashing it about one another, looking like so many butchers.*" As to Cumberland's part in the massacre, he may not have expressly ordered it, but he certainly took no steps to prevent it.

On Drummossie Moor died the last hope of the house of Stewart.

The Prince leaves Culloden

INDEX